MY CAMINO, MY LIFE

 A Sole to Soul Connection

MY CAMINO, MY LIFE

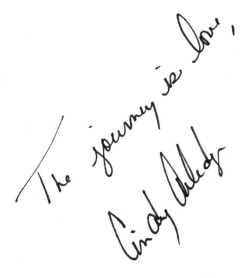 A Sole to Soul Connection

The journey is love,

Cindy Arledge

Cindy Arledge

Praise for
My Camino, My Life

"Cindy's humorous and inspiring story is a great read for anyone considering walking the Camino or seeking more out of life."

—John P. Strelecky, #1 best-selling author of
The Why Cafe

"Cindy shares her Camino journey in an exquisite authentic way. She provides the reader with key lessons learned about the Camino and human nature. Best of all, I loved her raw honesty."

—Lauren Midgley, Time Behaviorist and author of
It's 6 a.m. and I'm Already Behind

"I didn't know I needed the lessons, but they leapt from the pages and into my soul! I found myself smiling throughout the tale, and I could imagine myself right there with her. Cindy's insight and thoughts spoke to my heart and purpose."

—Brenna Smith, Founder and CEO
SheNOW, LLC

Praise for Cindy Arledge and
CUR$E OF INHERITANCE

"I speak from experience when I counsel you to read and take to heart what you learn from this book. Ignorance is not bliss when it comes to inheritance. Adopting this information will not only change your life, it will improve the entire dynamic of your family."

—Bobbi Schwartz, Founder and CEO of
Be Iconic Style

"My husband and I have been real estate investors for more than 20 years. We are all too familiar with the Cur$e of Inheritance. We've seen countless homes over the years owned by heirs of unplanned estates that end up in foreclosure or taken by the county for property taxes. The family ends up with broken relationships and no proceeds from what is often the most valuable portion of their loved one's estate. Over and over again they say, 'I never expected this from my siblings.'"

—Toni D'Angelo-Lott, HomeVestors,
We Buy Ugly Houses™ Franchisee

"It isn't often we get simple advice for complex problems, but Cindy Arledge has managed to succinctly navigate the complexities of inheritance. Whether you are the beneficiary of an inheritance or the benefactor, this is a must read for the entire family. She writes from the heart and mind, and is straight forward and full of empirical data."

—Kathy Miner, Award-winning 5-Star Realtor

MY CAMINO, MY LIFE
A Sole to Soul Connection

Pubished by:

Legacy Inheritance Partners, Ltd
5100 Eldorado Parkway, Suite 102-703
McKinney, TX 75070

1ST EDITION

Cover and Interior Design by Brian Moreland

clam symbol Fotolia © impressed-media.de
Camino de Santiago map graphic licensed from Shutterstock

Printed in the U.S.A.

ISBN 978-0-9826953-0-2

Disclaimer

This book provides information about the pilgrimage on the Camino de Santiago and life in general. It is sold with the understanding that the publisher and author are not engaged in rendering legal, accounting or other professional services. If legal or other expert assistance is required, the services of a competent professional should be sought.

Every effort has been made to make this book as complete and accurate as possible. However, there may be mistakes both typographical and in content. Therefore, this text should be used only as a general guide.

The purpose of this book is to educate and entertain. The author and GRIPP Productions, Ltd. shall have neither liability nor responsibility to any person or entity with respect to any loss or damage caused or alleged to be caused directly or indirectly by the information contained in this book.

If you do not wish to be bound by the above, you may return this book to the publisher for a full refund.

Acknowledgements

I wish to thank my husband, who sacrificed so much for me to achieve this dream and my family, who survived and thrived during difficult times while "Elmo" walked Spain. Thank you for your continued support while I completed the second journey of capturing my experience on paper.

My brother, Richard, who inspires me to stay true to my path.

My two *Dare to Dream* friends, Thom Ricks and Jodi Stauffer, who traveled halfway around the world to celebrate birthdays and to share this incredible experience.

Thanks to Kim Wallace and Linda Tom, for training with me, and Daryl Dancer, for your advice in clothing and packing options. The REI San Antonio staff was truly outstanding in outfitting me for this trip. In addition to excellent advice on my purchases, they provided encouragement. At REI, walking 500 miles isn't weird and I felt at home.

My appreciation for Yvonne Baca, Paul Rockwood and Mark LeBlanc, who generously answered so many questions about their Camino in preparation of mine.

Thank you to the Pilgrims who shared the path with me. I am grateful for the time we spent together. The memories are etched in my heart. Blessings to Sheelagh, Dennis, Becky and Dale. It is no accident that we met. Until I see you again, Buen Camino, dear soulmates.

In addition to those mentioned above, the following *Believing Mirrors* encouraged me to persevere: John P. Strelecky, the March Maui Tribe, Kat Wells, Matthews and McGuire, NSA North Texas, CPSisters, the Artist Way Tribe, Elaine Glass Rosenthal, Kate Delaney, Bill Bird, Brenna Jue, Mike C. Matthews, and Brian Moreland.

Contents

"A journey of a thousand miles begins with a single step."

—Lao Tzu

CAMINO DE SANTIAGO

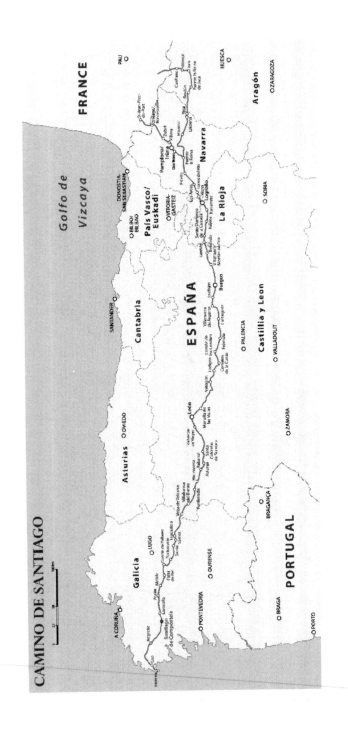

Introduction

Why did I walk the Camino? Why did I write this book? The reasons for both changed along the way. When I set out to walk the Camino, I left with the intention of testing a formula for empowerment that I spent more than a decade developing. I named it GRIPP Life™ and utilized it to transform my life to live "my best day ever," a life filled with gratitude and purpose.

My formula was born from the loss I experienced when my parents passed away within eight months of each other. My grief was compounded when my family was torn apart by my parents' end-of-life decisions. I had no idea how I had come to such a painful place, but I was determined to never live like a victim again.

Life isn't always pleasant—s&!t happens. And when s&!t happens, the GRIPP Life™ formula has provided me with the tools I needed to empower myself. To remain centered in my values during difficult situations. Situations that I had no control over. Like when my brother, Richard, was found guilty of conspiracy and sentenced to federal prison. He owned a car dealership. He refused to plead guilty and maintains his innocence. Standing firm in his truth came at a very high price. His refusal to confess added time onto his sentence. He is currently serving 16 years for a victimless crime. Victimless, according to the government report. GRIPP Life™ provided me with the tools to support my brother and continues to guide me in my relationship with him.

Then there's the time I borrowed millions of dollars to purchase commercial real estate to settle my parents' estate right BEFORE the 2008 market crash. GRIPP Life™ provided me with the tools to feel prosperous, despite the debt, and continues to guide me in my financial decisions.

Despite these successes and others, I had to be 100% sure they worked. I had the idea of conducting an experiment before sharing my formula with others. Ease and Grace are the cornerstones of the formula. *Ease* is where I co-create my future with the Universe and ask the Universe to pave the way. *Grace* is my acceptance of reality with the knowledge that no matter what happens it is for my highest good. What better way to test them than to complete a 500-mile Pilgrimage in Spain! Not only did I plan to complete my Pilgrimage, I set my intention to walk the 500 miles with Ease and Grace!

I became aware of the Camino after watching the movie *The Way*. If you haven't heard of the Camino, or don't know what it is, you are not alone. When I began planning my trip, I was very confused. There are multiple routes to the same destination and multiple names for just about everything.

In a nutshell, walking the Camino is an ancient Christian pilgrimage across Europe. All routes share a single destination: Santiago de Compostela (often shortened to "Santiago"). Santiago is located in the Galicia region of Spain. It is also known as "The Way of St. James," (often shortened to "The Way"). For centuries, Christians have walked the Camino to enrich their religious and spiritual life in harsh conditions.

I had not considered walking it until I heard Shirley MacLaine's interview with Oprah Winfrey. If Shirley could do it at 60, surely I could do it at 55. It wasn't too late for me.

But it wasn't until I completed John P. Strelecky's Discovery

Course that I decided to commit to walking the Camino and test GRIPP Life™ along the way. My dream was to write a book. The Camino was the path to this book.

When I set out to write a book about my adventure, I thought I knew what its content would be. After all, I developed the formula, identified the experiment and walked 500 miles. I thought the book would be my story of walking with Ease and Grace, inspiring you, the reader, to walk the Camino and GRIPP Life.

It is all those things and more. In sharing my story, I walked a second Camino. In the second Camino, the experiences from the first exponentially grew and influenced my life.

My writing sessions began with a prayer, followed by a review of my daily diary notes and looking at the photos taken on that day. In doing so, I became a scribe for the Creator. So much so, I often asked, "You want me to talk about *THAT? REALLY?!*" I was surprised where the words took me, but I obeyed.

Even when I didn't want to, I trusted the Voice. In doing so, I removed the mask and bared my soul. There is no place to hide. I am raw, vulnerable and real, and right where I'm supposed to be, living each day as a gift.

My Camino, My Life is the story of my 500-mile journey walking the Camino as well as my life, shared with the intention to inspire you to GRIPP LIFE and enjoy each day as a gift.

Cindy Arledge

Leaving Texas

San Antonio to Paris, France
8,312 km (5,165 miles)

After months of preparation and planning, I can't believe the day is finally here! After a restless night, my husband Gerald has loaded my backpack into the car and we're headed to San Antonio. We have one stop to make before the airport. Dr. Maller, my DDS pulled two teeth with failing root canals last December, and has graciously agreed to meet me at 7:30 this morning for one last treatment on the gaping hole in my gum. This was not the plan when the teeth were pulled in December. The plan was to have my new teeth implants installed before I left for the Camino.

But life doesn't always work out the way we plan. Of course, I'm not happy about the situation, but I'm not surprised either, because when I made the decision to pull the teeth, my body was screaming "NO!" My stomach was in a knot. I distinctly heard "This is not the right decision" and signed the medical release anyway. I ignored my Voice, internal guidance system, intuition, whatever you call the "inner knowing" inside of you. I didn't listen to the Voice because Gerald had two teeth pulled a few months before and it dramatically improved his health.

Three weeks before my departure, a "final check" appointment to clear me for my teeth implants turned into unexpected surgery to scoop out infected gum tissue. The gums had healed on the outside, but not the inside. It wasn't anybody's fault, things like this happen. Dr. Maller assured me that I could make my journey as planned and provided weekly treatments to aid the healing process.

After the gum treatment, Gerald and I head to the airport with plenty of time to spare. Which is good, because in spite of months of preparation, I still have work to do. My day job is managing commercial real estate partnerships, and despite my best efforts, several deals refused to come together. Our attorney has drawn up the necessary documents that authorize Gerald to act on my behalf while I'm gone, but I have a few more items to complete before I go. With only a few minutes to spare, I shut down my computer and say a quick goodbye. After months of preparation, I'm on my way.

My itinerary includes a plane change in Atlanta and then an overnight flight to Paris where I plan to catch a series of trains into Saint-Jean-Pied-de-Port, France (St. Jean or SJPP for short), the starting point of the Camino Frances.

My intention of walking the Camino with Ease and Grace is tested before my flight ever leaves the ground. The San Antonio to Atlanta flight is delayed due to a "reset button" error. Because of this, I miss my Atlanta flight to Paris. Upon landing in Atlanta, I receive a text that I've been automatically booked on a flight that leaves at 10:00 p.m. My problem with this flight is I won't arrive in Paris until the following afternoon, meaning I will miss my trains to St. Jean.

While the plane is taxiing to the gate in Atlanta, I'm busy on my phone checking out flight information. There are several leaving in a few hours, and I'm determined to be on one of them.

As soon as we pull into the gate, everyone rushes off the plane in an effort to make new connections. When life goes your way, it's easy to Trust. When it doesn't, the trick is to take action towards what you WANT, while letting go of the results. As I face the frazzled airline employee, I struggle to maintain my focus and remind myself, *She was not responsible for the delay. She is here to help me.*

After several tense moments of fingernails flying across the keyboard, and my continuous internal loop of *I am a Pilgrim, trust the journey,* a seat is found on the next flight that leaves in two hours. *Eureka!* My elation is short lived when I hear her say, "You will need to contact the luggage department about your two pieces of luggage to ensure they make your flight."

Uh oh, I only checked one bag. Did it multiply? Do I have someone else's bag? Did they inspect my bag and remove the poles to create a second bag? Will my bags make my flight?

I am a Pilgrim. I am a Pilgrim. I am a Pilgrim.

My layover in Atlanta zooms by and I board the plane for Paris with anticipation and appreciation. This is the biggest plane I've ever been on, and I'm amazed with its size. Having never flown a trans-Atlantic flight, I thought a window seat would be a great idea. The reality is quite different. Staying hydrated and being polite has proven challenging to my bladder. The Russian couple next to me do not sleep at the same time, either one or the other is asleep. I'm not a small person, and neither is the woman sitting next to me. Since we've been thigh to thigh for ten-plus hours, I wonder if I should send her a postcard.

My daily log from the plane reads: I made the flight, but am unsure of the status of my luggage. We are approximately 30 minutes away from Paris. It has been a long night, cramped, not able to sleep. Sat next to a nice Russian couple from Florida traveling to Moscow. Food has been good. Fed us twice . . . I am calm, serene and ready for this adventure. It doesn't seem real, in a nice kind of way. First class looks nice and comfy. At 38,000 feet, ice crystals form on the window on the inside. Who knew? Outside temperature is reading -79.6 degrees. No sleep, watched free movies, read and ready for the next stage of this journey.

Hello, Europe!

Paris to St. Jean, France
846 km (526 miles)

Now that my flight has landed and I'm in Paris, let me just say WOW! I am ready for the next leg of my adventure, navigating the Charles de Gaulle Airport to the train station. Despite dire warnings from several seasoned travelers, I'm determined to find my way, purchase my ticket and begin the next stage of my journey without being the victim of pickpockets or rude natives. I'm relying on the twinkle in my eye, a genuine smile and the energy of good will to speak for me. My mantra is "I am safe. All is well."

Following the crowd to the baggage claim, I'm relieved to retrieve one bag in perfect condition. I remove my pack from the cover, strap it to my back and breeze through customs. So far, so good. Now, to find my way to the train station.

I've discovered a tricky way to sidestep the "rude" prediction. I don't ask for help or talk to anyone. Instead, I follow the signs to the station. The kiosks in the train lobby are, of course, written in French and I'm forced to break my silence. The information desk woman is neither rude nor kind as she directs me to the queue to purchase a train ticket.

Standing in the crowded queue, listening to the multitude of languages coursing around me is humbling. My European journey has just begun and I'm already feeling distressed. I'm in awe of the courage it must take to immigrate to a foreign land, especially when seeking asylum. Counting my blessings that my situation is temporary, I'm brought back to gratitude, the foundation of enjoying a life of Ease and Grace.

I can read a clock in any language, and after 20-plus minutes of no progression in the queue, I realize I won't make the train to Biarritz. Time to pivot. Turning to leave, I gift my ticket number to the guy behind me who looks confused by my sudden departure.

I schlep my way back to the terminal, purchase an Easy Jet airline ticket, have time to enjoy a delicious lunch and find my gate with time to spare. By making this change, I realize that I will arrive in Biarritz several hours faster than if I'd taken the train. If the next leg of my journey goes as easy as the first two, I'll be walking the Camino tomorrow!

At the gate, I spot my first group of Pilgrims. I think of them as the Paris Pilgrims, because that is where I met them. Even though we're strangers, we greet each other like long lost family members. Excitedly, we discuss plans to share a ride from the Biarritz airport to the train station. The train will take us from Biarritz to St. Jean, the starting point of the Camino.

Everything feels surreal. I imagine myself stepping off the train in a swirl of fog and mist, just like Martin Sheen in the movie *The Way*. Never mind that the sun is shining, and it will be early afternoon when we arrive; it isn't time for a reality check.

Standing in line to board the plane, I notice everyone else's backpacks are small enough to carry on the plane. *Hmm, I guess they didn't bring a pocket knife.* During the short flight, I mentally review the items in my pack and wonder what I could have left at home. As we exit the plane, I tell the others to go on, that I'll join them after I retrieve my pack. Standing in the tiny baggage claim area, I feel like a kid in a candy store, absorbing the moment. I'm drawn to a tall blonde removing her backpack from a suitcase. She's quickly joined by two petite brunettes, also wearing backpacks, and I surmise that another group of Pilgrims has found each other.

Instinctively I know I need to join this group. As soon as my bag lumbers down the ramp, I grab it and lug it towards the trio of women. After a quick introduction, it becomes clear that the blonde, Sheelagh from Ireland, is a leader that we should follow. She has done her research and it seems my beloved train is currently closed for track construction. First reality check: no misty train exit for me in St. Jean.

The four of us decide to share a taxi to St. Jean. As we climb into the cab, out of the corner of my eye, I see the Paris Pilgrims waiting for the bus. I wave as I get into the cab, but I'm unsure if anyone sees me.

The taxi weaves its way past towering trees, huge rocks, and flowing streams on winding roads. I'm reminded of the Colorado Rockies. The four of us chat during the hour-plus trip. The brunettes are mother and daughter from Canada. Louise, the mother, has been planning her Camino for quite some time. Her daughter, Ashley, joined her at the last moment. Sheelagh's departure date for her Camino was delayed several times, and for several reasons, including an airline strike. I am in no doubt that we've been brought together by Universal forces to meet each other and share this ride.

Coming around a sharp left turn, we enter St. Jean and the car comes to a screeching halt in the middle of the road. Huh? To my left is a modern shopping strip center and to my right is a café and more shopping. This wasn't in the movie *The Way*. I know, because I watched it a few days before my departure. Where are the quaint buildings with the wooden shutters and doors? Where are the narrow cobblestone streets?

The driver points us to the right and wishes us *"Buen Camino."* Buen Camino is the standard greeting for Pilgrims and can be used for just about anything, including "hello," "goodbye," "hope you make it."

Following the driver's instructions, we head towards the right, and in a single block find ourselves in another century. The Rue de la Citadelle is everything I had dreamed of and more. The street is quiet. A dog trots past us, confident and purposeful, as if on a mission. The cobblestone streets, so beautiful and quaint, are actually hard on the knees and feet.

I stop to take it all in. It's so quiet I can hear the sound of water gurgling in the sewer pipes. Until the church bells ring, their clangs obliterating all other sounds. Stone buildings rise above me on both sides, making the road seem narrower than it is. With Sheelagh in the lead, we squeeze past a parked truck in search of the Pilgrim office.

We've arrived in St. Jean during siesta, which explains the quiet street and the closed Pilgrim office. The office won't open for another thirty minutes, so we use the time to find a bed for the night. Like a small group of penguins, we make our way down Rue de Citadelle. A "Welcome Pilgrim" sign is all it takes to convince us to stay in the municipal *alburgue* (hostel).

After completing the paperwork, we're shown a large room filled with red bunk beds. Our penguin pack scatters and claims beds on opposite sides of the room. We unpack our packs then head back to the Pilgrim office to obtain our credential.

Every Pilgrim needs a credential. It is your passport for discounted food and your ticket for a place to sleep each night. Like a passport, Pilgrims need to have their credential stamped and dated, at least once a day. Most villages, but not all, offer at least one place for Pilgrims to spend the night. Depending on the size of the town or its location, Pilgrims usually have a choice that ranges from sleeping on a mat on the floor among a group of people to a comfy bed in a room by yourself, and everything in between. Prices vary accordingly. During the busy summer season, it is a daily race for a bed, which is why I'm walking in

April.

The Pilgrim office charges two euro for a credential and imprints the first *sello* (stamp). You can also obtain a specially designed plastic bag to protect your credential from the rain, if you know to ask for one, or if the Pilgrim volunteer likes you. I didn't fit into either one of these categories.

With my stamped credential, I am now an official Pilgrim, yea! Sheelagh, Louise and Ashley get theirs too. Leaving the Pilgrim office, we see that siesta is over and the shops are open. I purchase a patch to have sewn on the top of my backpack. We drift from shop to shop and visit the Church of Our Lady at the End of the Bridge. I'm blown away by the majesty of the church.

My new friends suggest more exploration of St. Jean, but I'm feeling the need to be alone. I go back to the alburgue to shower, wash socks and underwear. With refreshed body and clothes swinging in the wind, I head out to explore the town on my own. Feeling utterly ridiculous in pink Crocs, shorts and compression socks, I stroll down the cobblestone streets to hire a seamstress to sew my patch.

Afterward, I find a café to enjoy a celebratory glass of champagne and contemplate tomorrow's journey.

On my way back to the alburgue, I make a last minute decision to purchase a wide brimmed purple hat and some hat pins. I'm concerned that the cap I brought won't protect my ears or neck.

My daily log reads: I took care of myself tonight. Shower, washed clothes, foot treatment. My gums bled when I brushed my teeth. I wonder, is that good or bad? Who knows? I'm feeling optimistic about the trip tomorrow (Expecting—Is this a mistake?—an easy day). Buen Camino! It only takes a slight shift and some focus to elevate your life. It is the difference between taking a walk and walking the Camino.

St. Jean, France

PART ONE

Walking with Angels

"In each moment I sense my guides setting up situations for me to learn the next lesson. I have an image of adoring angels urging me to learn through grace rather than grit."

—Brierley Camino de Santiago Guide Book

Day 1

Stage 1 - St. Jean to Orrison, France
7.8 km (4.85 miles)

I was hoping for a good night's sleep since it has been two days since I slept in a bed. But multiple trips to the bathroom last night and anticipation for the day has me up before dawn, and unrested. The first morning trip down steep stone steps to a bathroom next to a room full of snoring men is a bust. The second trip up a flight of steps to a secluded bathroom is successful.

During my research, I read several stories about toilet paper litter on the Camino, and I was determined to not be a part of the problem. My intention before leaving was to only use indoor plumbing. For me, it is a matter of respecting the land. Just in case, I've packed an emergency portable bathroom kit that consists of a small pack of baby wipes and several small baggies carried inside a large baggie. This is a light-weight item that I never intend to use, but knowing that it's there, if I need it, gives me oodles of confidence.

Since I can't sleep, I might as well get up and go. There's no need to toss and turn in bed, not when I can be walking and experiencing the Camino. Truth is there's no hurry to leave, because my destination is only 8 km away. Yesterday, while receiving my credential, the Pilgrim office made a reservation for me at the Orrison alburgue. Orrison is the place to stay if you don't want to make the arduous trip to Roncesvalles, which I don't. Walking 20+ km on my first day does not fit into my plan of Ease and Grace. I suspect making it to Orrison will be all I can do for my first day on the trail.

After a traditional breakfast of dry toast and tea, served in a bowl instead of a cup, I'm ready to hit the trail. Except it's still dark. Other Pilgrims are on the road, some in a hurry, others, like me, appear to be waiting until it's light outside before leaving the security of St. Jean. I'm asked to take a picture of two Pilgrims, and they return the favor. Despite all my research, I have no idea what to expect. I say a prayer and then begin walking. Rather than stress, I feel calm knowing that I am cared for, just as I am.

The trail leading out of St. Jean begins as an ancient road that turns into a modern roadway and climbs through a residential area. My pace is slow and I'm passed by everybody. Despite the occasional yellow arrows pointing the way, the Pilgrims who've passed me disappear in the uphill turns, and I'm unsure of where to go. I stop frequently to check my guidebook.

As I pass through the residential area, I see a construction crane and stop to take a picture. These cranes were once known as the state bird of Texas and represent growth and abundance to me. I giggle, recognizing my weirdness, and enjoy taking the time to capture an image that has meaning to me.

One phenomenon that I'm beginning to notice is that I'm often two steps short from capturing the best photo, spotting the yellow arrow, or finding my way. With this awareness, I recognize my lesson for the day: Take two steps past my comfort zone.

My only stop of the day is at a café in Hunto, just 5 km from St. Jean. The café has a beautiful view of St. Jean with few customers sitting outside. Before leaving my pack and walking sticks next to the others leaning against a wall, I remove the racquetball from my pack. I sit down, remove my shoes and begin rolling my feet against the ball. "It hurts so good" is my mantra. The pain is short lived, as the tendons in my feet begin to stretch and relax. In the weeks leading up to this journey, I endured twice weekly Airrosti treatments for my feet and was instructed to stretch my feet at least three times a day and ice them as often as possible. After spending $1,000 for these painful treatments, I intend to follow instructions.

Enjoying the view, I eat my second breakfast consisting of eggs, bread and juice. The sounds of crows and woodpeckers compete with the more subtle buzzing of wood bees and wind rustling through the trees. I know it's time to go but I'm not ready yet, so I order my first cup of the famous coffee de leche and remember to obtain a sello for my credential.

The elevation from Hunto to Orrison is significantly steeper and has changed from road to natural path. The views of pastoral green pastures and herds of sheep go largely unnoticed. My goal is to breathe. Twelve steps and three breaths. Twelve steps and three breaths. When I do notice my surroundings, the loop in my head is "Ouch, ouch, ouch, oh, look at that. Ouch, ouch, ouch, oh, look at that."

The weather is perfect and I continue to take my time to Orrison. The Canadian taxi-sharing mom, Louise, catches up with me, and we walk together for a short while. Her daughter, Ashley, is walking a faster pace ahead of us. Louise is hurting significantly but remains committed to meet Ashley in Roncesvalles today and hurries up the trail.

I arrive in Orrison around noon to the sight of Louise completing yoga stretches in preparation for the second leg of her journey. I'm exhausted, grateful that I'm stopping for the day, and wish her "Buen Camino."

Room check-in has been suspended to serve lunch, so I enjoy a third breakfast, along with a tall beer to celebrate my arrival. After lunch, check-in resumes and I'm shown to my bed.

Outside stairs lead up to rooms above and behind the restaurant. My room has three bunk beds and I'm given the last available bed, an upper bunk on the left side of the room. My five roommates are all women. Two hail from France, one from England, one from Germany and Sheelagh from Ireland, with me representing Texas, um, the United States.

Remembering last night's double foray to the facilities, I'm daunted by the idea of climbing in and out of the upper bunk, and my face must show it. Sue from England is completing her second Camino and graciously offers her lower bunk to me. Gratefully, I accept and begin to find a place to store my things in the already crowded room. "Thank you, Sue!"

During check-in I was given an odd-shaped coin that would provide five minutes of hot water for the shower. Standing naked in the shower, without my glasses, trying to fit the coin into the machine is quite the adventure. After several fumbling attempts, the coin drops into the machine with a *clink*. And then, nothing. Looking around, I notice a button under the faucet, push it and am rewarded with semi-warm water. Satisfied about my progress, I remove the special soap leaves to begin washing my hair. I'm utterly unprepared for the water to stop in a minute. Pressing the button, I'm relieved when the water begins again. When the water cuts off after another minute, I understand that five minutes is five one-minute increments of water usage. I manage my soap/rinse shower accordingly, praying that I've counted to five correctly.

My clothing choices include three long-sleeve shirts, two walking pants and pajamas, which consist of a pair of yoga pants and a short-sleeved shirt. Now that I'm clean, wearing pajamas is the logical choice. No one needs to know, except me. I hand wash my underwear and socks then head out to the clothes line to hang them to dry. The wind is blowing fiercely, and many Pilgrims' clothes are on the ground. After securing my clothes with my large safety pins, I pick up and re-hang the clothes I find on the ground and say a silent prayer of gratitude to Yvonne, my friend who advised me to bring safety pins.

A nap is next on the agenda, but stomach cramps prevent any enjoyment of resting. A long visit to the facilities relieves the ache in my belly, and I focus on putting this sickness behind me. Tomorrow's stage is twice as long as today's stage, and there are no services available. I dread the idea of busting out the portable toilet on the second day with a sick tummy.

Rather than dwell on my upset stomach, I head downstairs to spend time with my fellow Pilgrims until dinner. A meal that I'm unsure if I should eat or not. Wearing my coat over my pajamas to stay warm in the cool mountain air, I see Sheelagh and join her and an American couple.

Pilgrim dinner at the Orrison alburgue is a unique experience. Since it's the first stop for Pilgrims beginning the Camino in St. Jean, the owners ask everyone to stand up, introduce themselves and say where they're from. The owners point towards my side of the room. My table mates look at each other, asking the unspoken question, "Who wants to go first?" In the face of indecisiveness, my commander (it's one of my strengths according to StrengthsFinder

2.0) takes over. "Hello, I'm Cindy Arledge and I'm from Texas."

Next up are Baly and Jose, a darling married couple from California that I had felt connected to in Paris. They were a part of the Paris Pilgrim group whom I last saw in Biarritz waiting for their bus. We have happily reunited at dinner and share our stories of how we arrived in St. Jean. Their tale of two bus rides and a later arrival in St. Jean is a big *yes* for trusting the Voice. More importantly, seeing them again, so soon on the trip, reinforces our connection. During my research, I heard story after story of this reuniting of friends, and on day one, I'm experiencing it.

When they stand up to introduce themselves and say where they're from, they say "the States," as does every other American in the group. Oops, this Texan, like all others I know, certainly has pride in our state and, to be fair, at one point in our history we were our own country.

My stomach is feeling better, but I'm tentative with my food choices. Rather than drink the wine, I request water. The three-course Pilgrim dinner is delicious and ends with my favorite Camino dessert, the Santiago cake. This dense almond cake has the symbol of the Camino stenciled on top with powdered sugar.

The room is full to capacity, and after the meal the alburgue staff scurries to pick up dishes. Having read the suggestions from my guidebook to be helpful, I offer to clear the table and compliment the chef, Jean-Jacques. He seems overjoyed by the compliment and gives me a hug and kiss-kiss in return.

Everyone returns to their room to get ready for bed. I stretch my feet on my racquetball, and the German checks her feet for blisters and rubs lotion on them. Seeing us, our experienced English roommate says, "I forgot about the obsession with feet."

Each night I write in two notebooks, my daily log to capture the day's activities and my prosperity notebook, which is a logbook of every dollar I spend. From past experience, I know that a daily journal is the only way to capture the moment, and I'm dedicated to capturing this journey.

For the past six years, I've participated in an Artist's Way group. We study at least three books each year, one chapter per week, and meet for several hours to discuss the chapter. We call ourselves the Artist Way Tribe. Our time together is sacred, meaning what is said in the group stays in the group. Typically, we begin each year by studying *The Artist's Way* by Julia Cameron. From there, we decide on our next book to study. Before starting a new book, we invite others to join us, but after week two or three, close the group to new people for the duration of the book.

Several years ago, we added Julia Cameron's book *The Prosperous Heart* to our annual rotation. We have three weeks left to complete the book, so I will be participating via our private Facebook page. The impact of this particular book over the past three years has been immense for Gerald and me, which is why I plan to participate with my study group while walking the Camino. I've downloaded *The Prosperous Heart* to the Kindle app on my phone so that I can read my weekly chapter.

A large part of the impact this study provides comes from daily counting the money you spend. Rather than think of it as spending, I think of it as investing in my life. In reviewing today's prosperity notebook, I may have found the cause of my earlier tummy issue. It's a tossup between three breakfasts or the beer with the last one.

Tomorrow, we will cross the Pyrenees Mountains into Spain, following the path that Napoleon used to lead his troops. Word is, there is still snow on the ground. Day one on the Camino has been a success. Today, I learned to take two steps past my comfort zone.

Day 2

Stage 1 - Orrison, France to Roncesvalles, Spain
17.3 km (10.75 miles)

The day starts abruptly when Sue unceremoniously turns on the light. I'm disoriented for a heartbeat then my cheeks flame with embarrassment, as memories from the night before flood my consciousness. I apologize again to the French woman across from me, but she remains unmoved. With cutting eyes, in rapid fire French, she must be telling her friend how I tried to get in bed with her last night. The rest of my roommates are clueless to the event and don't understand what is being said, but the tension in the room is palatable.

It was an honest mistake, really. At approximately 11:30 p.m. my bladder requested a trip to the bathroom. Unfortunately, my phone was charging across the room, and I forgot to put my headlamp next to the bed. I remember thinking, *It's a simple box, Cindy. You know where your bed is in respect to the door. Just use the bunks to follow the wall and work your way around. Come on, you can do it. OK, here goes. Uh, oh. Where am I? Shouldn't I be at the door by now? What is this indention? Guess I better get back to my bed and start over.*

Unfortunately, the bed I returned to wasn't mine and the French woman in it FREAKED OUT. I don't blame her. I was freaked out too. She quickly turned on her lamp.

"I am so sorry," I said. "I was trying to make it to the bathroom and got confused."

In two steps, I was back to my bed, sitting on the edge. She turned out her light, muttering in the dark.

Great, I'm back where I started, except now I have someone who hates me.

I continued to whisper "I am so sorry" in the darkness.

After what felt like forever, the French woman took pity on me and turned on her lamp so I could retrieve my headlamp from my pack. I made it to the bathroom without additional drama.

Note to self: Getting in someone else's bed does not make you popular on the Camino.

For my non-French roommates, I share my side of the story. Amid the laughter, everyone gets ready for the day. I notice our German roommate folding individual items with surgical precision and placing them in individual baggies. Curious, I question her on this system and discover it is her first line of defense to prevent bedbugs. Hmmmm, fascinating.

After filling up my Platypus water hydration system, I realize my pack is too full to fit the platypus back in its pouch. So I remove the majority of my stuff and toss it on the bed. Then I put my pack on the floor to wrestle the platypus into its place. As I turn around to begin shoving my stuff back into my pack, I step into a quickly growing puddle of water. To my horror, I discover that my water bottle's unclosed valve has leaked. More hating eyes penetrate me as I do my best to wipe up the puddle before anyone else steps in it. Hiking the Pyrenees in the snow never looked so good. I can't wait to get out of here.

Breakfast is self-serve: toast, coffee, juice and water. The camaraderie from the night before is gone, replaced with serious faces and deep thought. As for me, the need to separate myself from last night's embarrassment and this morning's wet-floor escapade is paramount.

I escape Orrison around 8:15, hitting the trail by myself. The wind is so fierce I feel like I'm being pushed backwards. It rains and then it stops. When it stops, the rain gear is too hot to wear, so I stop to remove my rain coat and pants. The poncho doesn't work well in the wind, because it blows like a parachute, pulling me backwards even more. The equipment is all new to me, and I'm searching for the best combination that will keep me dry without overheating. Poncho on, poncho off. Raincoat on, raincoat off. Rain pants on, rain pants off. Hot/cold. Wet/dry.

The trail is much more difficult today, and I'm glad that I split this stage into two parts. I can't imagine how Louise made it yesterday. At the top of a mountain, after a long steep uphill climb, I'm greeted by an Australian girl who kindly shares a bite of her favorite Australian chocolate with all who happen by. It's just the boost I need to keep going.

Sheelagh catches up to me and we walk part of the day together. Actually, her pace is much faster than mine, but since I don't stop to pee on the trail, we cross paths many times. She showers me with empathy and understanding about my Orrison mishaps. As we near the top of the mountain, we hit snow and decide to stick together. The trail is treacherous and it feels safer with a buddy.

Our entry into Spain is a bit of a letdown, a non-event. There is no border crossing or fanfare to let you know you have just entered another country.

The hard part of the journey today is not the climb, it is the descent. Coming off the snow, there is some question of which trail to take into Roncesvalles. Initially, Sheelagh and I set off on the less steep path, but quickly decide to turn around and follow the other Pilgrims. The alternative path is not well marked and it isn't worth getting lost in the woods.

Downhill is brutal and my guidebook warns that this is the section where many people injure themselves. The trail is steep, wet and slick and seems to go on forever. We meet a Pilgrim who

Sheelagh knows. He offers us a sugar cube, and we spend time enjoying his company and resting. The sugar tastes delicious and gives us the energy we need to continue the downward hike.

As we edge our way closer to our destination, Sheelagh and I agree that sharing a hotel room is preferable to the famous 180-bed monastery in Roncesvalles. We agree to split the cost and look forward to reaching sanctuary. "Brilliant move" sounds delightful in an Irish accent. I couldn't agree more.

We arrive in Roncesvalles around 3:45, find the hotel and check into our room. Ravenous, we head to the bar for a beer and a snack. Bar on the Camino doesn't have the same meaning as bar in the United States. Yes, it serves alcohol. It also serves food and is the local gathering place. Siesta is an important part of this culture, and the daily dose of connection in the afternoon is something to commend. We see a man named Allen and meet two Dutch Pilgrims. Sheelagh catches up with an Irish friend while I purchase a small baggie of ice cubes to soak my aching feet. While up in the room, I had already figured out that if I sat on the toilet, I could soak my feet in the bidet. I share my plans for the ice. The Danish men are amused.

While Sheelagh enjoys her friend and catches up on Facebook, I enjoy the solitude of the room. The bidet works beautifully to relieve my aching feet. Another Camino first.

Our Pilgrim dinner begins at 7:00 p.m. and consists of spaghetti, pork, French fries and rice pudding. A bargain at 10 euros. Sheelagh sits at another table and meets an incredible 79-year-young woman from Denver.

At my table, a nice couple from Nashville, walking their second Camino, share their wisdom and several gifts. Hal, a private detective, captivates us with entertaining stories. I share my creative use of the bidet, to the amusement of my table companions. Hal's wife gives every woman at the table a pair of handmade shell earrings. Hearing my tale of foot woe, my new

Tennessee friend gifts me with a jar of foot cream that she just purchased. Desperate to feel better, I gladly accept the foot cream and thank her for the gifts.

After dinner, Sheelagh stays behind to catch up on Facebook in the bar. It's the only place, besides a small landing area on the stairs, that we can connect to the Internet. I take the opportunity to enjoy a luxurious hot bath and do laundry. In the process, I discover that somehow I picked up extra laundry soap leaves but lost my hand soap leaves. And my poncho cover is nowhere to be found.

I string my dripping clothes between a chair and a chest and use my poncho to protect the wood floor. It's after 9:00 p.m. when we finely get to sleep.

Today, I learned how to breathe and walk.

Buen Camino, Day 2.

Day 3

Stage 2 - Roncesvalles to Viskarret
11.8 km (7.33 miles)

Finally, a goodnight's sleep! Sharing a room with one person with easy access to a private bathroom is infinitely more restful than sleeping in a room full of people and all the midnight bathroom issues. Even though my feet still hurt, the rest of me feels rejuvenated.

Breakfast is served at 8:00 a.m., so I've set my phone alarm for 7:30. At home, I'm not a morning person, but here on the Camino, I'm eager to start each day, and I find myself wide awake before daylight, again.

Last night, Sheelagh and I decided to walk together today to Viskarret, a mere 11.8 km away. After yesterday's long hike, up and down the Pyrenees, we're both ready for a day of Ease and Grace. I am grateful for her presence on my Camino, and I recognize that Sheelagh is a gift from the Universe.

After breakfast, we visit the Royal Collegiate Church of Saint Mary to obtain a stamp for our credentials, with the misguided hope of touring the facilities. We receive the stamp, but are denied access to the monastery by the warden, or *hospitalera*. She is responsible for running the facility, and her staff is too busy preparing for tonight's Pilgrims to grant us a tour. We enjoy a conversation with her about the impact that the movie *The Way* has had on the Camino and discover her sister had a small part in the movie, and the character of the hospitalera in Roncesvalles was based on her. Sheelagh and I peek into the courtyard, and agree that, although beautiful, our hotel last night was a better choice for us.

Standing outside the hotel, waiting for Sheelagh to make one last pit stop, I'm asked to take a picture of a trio of women in front of the "Santiago, 790 km" sign. They are three generations—grandmother, daughter and granddaughter—from San Antonio, Texas, celebrating the granddaughter's graduation from college. I hope to follow their example and in the future walk the Camino with my daughters and grandchildren. Meeting these beautiful women from San Antonio connects me to home, and I am comforted by their presence. It feels like a cosmic kiss of encouragement at the start of my day.

It's 10:00 a.m. before we officially set out, and we're the only Pilgrims for as far as I can see. After taking a selfie together with the 790 km sign, we set out down the trail. After yesterday, it's a breeze. The single wide track is easy to follow and takes us into the "Witches Woods." The diversity of the forest is incredible. At times I'm reminded of the forest around Lake Tahoe, and at others I feel like I'm in North Carolina. The variation of vegetation is incredible, breathtaking and entirely different from yesterday.

Leaving Roncesvalles late means we have the Camino to ourselves, and we're in no hurry. We stop often to take pictures, explore an empty underground house and talk, laugh and learn about each other. Sheelagh loves the idea of Ease and Grace and is embracing it wholeheartedly.

In Burguete, just 3 km from Roncesvalles, we make our first stop of the day at a welcoming café. Our breakfast at the hotel had not been that great, and after wandering around Roncesvalles before heading out, Burguete is a good place to refuel, stretch my feet and enjoy indoor plumbing.

The longer we're on the trail, the more people pass us, mainly men. One actually slows down to walk with us, and we learn that he started the day in St. Jean! Wow. Sheelagh and I are on day 3 and he is still on day 1. As we walk, we talk and come upon the subject of what we packed for the journey. He's carrying a selfie stick, something I had considered, but decided to leave at home. He whips it out and the three of us take a photo together to capture the moment.

Nearing Espinal, we come to a stream with a nice place to put hurting feet in ice-cold water. Just what my feet ordered! Sheelagh and our new companion join me in this respite. We share snacks from our packs, enjoy the beauty of our surroundings and our time together. When our feet soaking is done, our speedy Pilgrim gives us a hug and continues on his journey.

As Sheelagh and I near Viskarret, occasional Pilgrims continue to pass us. My favorite is the jogger wearing running shorts and a tiny day pack. He waves as he passes us, leaving us in the dust of his footprints. But like a mirage, several minutes later, we see him jogging towards us. He mentions a closed gate and is back asking for directions. We show him the map, that we're on the right trail. He doesn't know what to do at the gate, so he matches his pace to ours, his body language screaming, "Hurry up!"

When we reach the gate, we open it, walk through it, motion our jogger friend to follow us and close it behind us, while maintaining a straight face. He is still only long enough for us to snap a quick photo, then thanks us, and he's off like a rabbit. Pilgrims pass through many gates on the Camino. Just follow the basic rule of putting things back the way you find them and you will be fine. Between the tortoise and the hare, we definitely identify with the tortoise. After meeting the jogging Pilgrim, we name ourselves "the Tortugas," or turtles of the Camino.

It takes us 6 hours to reach Viskarret. We are traveling at the blazing speed of 2 km per hour. The day has been one of Ease and Grace, which builds my confidence in my ability to succeed on this journey. I am practicing self-care, which is a new concept for me. Having spent a lifetime of caring for others, my children, my parents and my spouses (Gerald is my third husband), the Camino is my opportunity to focus on taking care of myself.

With my newfound confidence, I am ready to pick up the pace so I can reach Santiago on schedule. Using the 33 stages in my John Brierley guidebook, I created three benchmarks to measure my progress while on my journey. By adding two extra days to each of the three sections, I have 39 days to complete the Camino. Prior to leaving home for this journey, I gave myself permission to make any adjustments to meet my benchmarks, including taking a bus or cab.

To qualify for a *compostela*, the certificate of completion written in Latin, a Pilgrim need only walk the final 100 km of the route into Santiago. So why am I starting my Camino in St. Jean, an extra 690 km from Santiago? My suspicion is that the Camino is like earning my Bachelor's and Master's degrees as a single mom. It is the knowledge that I received in pursuit of the diploma that changed my life, not the diploma itself. The diploma merely represents confirmation of the energy I put forth to earn it and the wisdom I received along the way.

Utilizing benchmarks to mark my progress on the Camino and giving myself permission to be flexible during the first two-thirds of my journey allow me to focus on what matters, taking it a day at a time without judging myself as being *less than others* for taking care of myself along the way.

Our goal for the night is La Posada Hotel, which is the same name as the hotel we stayed in last night. However, La Posada in Roncesvalles was a three-star hotel, and this La Posada is a *casa rural* (country house). Big difference. Our hospitalera is less than enthusiastic in her welcome to us. She seems put off by our joviality. Although it looks like we're the only ones here, she shows us a room on the top floor. Up five flights of stairs! Our room is nice; we have two beds and a private bathroom again, but the vibe of the place is unwelcoming and cold.

The cost of sharing a room with Sheelagh is very affordable, and the benefits are tremendous. Laundry service is available for an extra charge, and both Sheelagh and I take advantage of the opportunity of clean clothes. Up to this point, hand washing my clothes with the soap leaves in a sink of cold water has not been producing that clean feeling that a machine wash can provide.

At our Pilgrim meal, we meet the one additional guest staying at La Posada—Andrea from Italy. He has walked all the way from St. Jean to Viskarret today! He walked in one day what it took Sheelagh and me three days to accomplish. Andrea's ability to walk almost 45 km on his first day is quite a feat. While it's not something I want to do, I celebrate his achievement.

During dinner, our hospitalera comments that Andrea is a "real Pilgrim," implying that Sheelagh and I do not qualify. During our dinner conversation, we discover that Andrea was charged two euros less for this meal than we're paying. For just a moment, I burn with the unjust judgment that is affecting my pocketbook and consider requesting a refund.

I quickly recognize the burn as a symptom of giving my power away. The burn means I am allowing someone else's opinion of me to interrupt my peace of mind. It's not her judgment of me that's causing the burn; it is me giving away my power that has created the turmoil. Rather than taking action to ask for a refund, I take action to regain my peace. She is not the first person to judge me and won't be the last. Feeling the burn and recognizing it for what it really is bring me to gratitude for the fine meal and company and the reminder lesson that the hospitalera has provided.

After dinner, Andrea, Sheelagh and I set out in search of ice to soak my feet. There is a bidet calling my name. Unfortunately, it seems there is no ice to be found in the entire village. I can't tell if the withering looks I'm receiving are in response to my horrible

Spanish, or the request for ice. We head back to the sitting room on the fifth floor of our casa rural. It is the best place to access Wi-Fi (pronounced "we-fee" in Spain). Sheelagh introduces me to an app called "WhatsApp" and gives me her number so we can continue to communicate while on the Camino. The three of us friend each other, update our Facebook pages and use Andrea's selfie stick to capture the memory of our great evening together. In addition, I send an email to my brother, complete my Prosperous Heart Prosperity homework and text Gerald my location and status.

Our clothes are returned by our hostess wearing her disapproving frown. Although our day has been relatively easy, we are tired. After a delightful bath, I'm ready for bed. Tomorrow is a new day. I'm eager to see what it will bring and ready to pick up my pace. Today's gift has been Sheelagh, a friend with whom to enjoy Ease and Grace.

Email to my brother, Richard:

Hello from Spain!

You are with me every step of the way.

Love you,
Cindy

Day 4

Stage 2 – Viskarret to Larrasoaña
15.6 km (9.7 miles)

No need for an alarm clock on the Camino. I'm up and ready to go as usual, before daylight. The last few days have given me the confidence I need to push myself a little harder to reach my first benchmark, and I'm ready to hit the trail. Sheelagh, on the other hand, is snuggled deep under the covers and in no hurry to leave. Confident we will see each other again, I decide to set out on my own. But first, I have to get out of this casa rural.

By headlamp, I navigate the five flights of creaky stairs in my pink crocs, doing my best to be quiet. At the bottom of the stairs, I remove my backpack, gather my walking shoes and sticks, sit down on the wooden bench and change shoes. After attaching my crocs to the outside of my backpack, I sling it over my left shoulder into place. One of the features I love about my backpack is the ability to remove the top section and use it as a belly pack, which I prefer to do because it takes weight from my back and redistributes it to the front. And it's so encouraging to look down and see my Camino patch.

Time for the daily pat-down. Starting from the top: Hat. Check. Passport. Check. Belly pack. Check. Phone in right leg pocket. Check. Daily journal in left pocket. Check. Walking sticks. Check.

With everything in place, I make the last turn into the foyer and my heart sinks. Our casa rural is, in fact, a fortress in disguise. The medieval version of a zombie door barricade stands between me and freedom. Two giant wooden doors form an arch and are secured by a wooden beam resting inside two metal brackets. I see that the left side is a Dutch door with at least three latches that opens up God knows what. Intimidated by the hardware, I seek an easier exit through the dining room. The door to the outside is a simple glass door but secured by a dead bolt that requires a key. A key that my less-than-friendly hospitalera owns.

I have two options: one, retreat upstairs until the sun comes up, or two, tackle the monstrosity of a door. Not one to give up easily, I remove my backpack and lean it, with my walking sticks, in the corner. It's going to take both hands and some strength to lift the wooden beam from its metal supports. I gently place it on the floor against the wall and then, starting at the top, begin to twist and turn latches.

The first latch releases the top half of the Dutch door. With a moan it swings towards my head like a club. I duck for safety and, I catch it before it hits the wall. Whew! Just dodged a close one. Last thing I want to do is wake up an angry hospitalera. Next latch opens the bottom half of the Dutch door with a *cha-chink, clank,* and *whoosh*. As the sounds ricochet off the rock floor and walls, I freeze and hold my breath. Do I make a run for it or remain still? The door to HER room is next to the front door. When it remains closed, I relax and prepare to make a hasty exit.

I quickly gather my backpack and sticks and move them outside. I re-latch the bottom of the Dutch door and pull the top one closed.

It's 6:15 in the morning and I've successfully escaped from my first fortress!

One more swing of the backpack, another pat-down, and I'm ready to go. As I set out into the inky blackness, guided by the light of my headlamp, I experience an equipment failure—my glasses are fogging up from the mist created by my own breath. I wipe them several times to no avail. Might as well take them off. I can't see anyway.

I expected it to be quiet this early in the morning, but it's not. The ringing of horse bells declares their restlessness in the pre-dawn hour. The birds are invisible cheerleaders, urging me down the trail. And the Voice, my Intuition, is urging me to utilize this valuable time to cover some distance. Although I can only see a few feet in front of me, I feel safe. I wonder what beautiful vistas I'm missing. I trust my Voice and keep walking.

It's still dark when I reach Lintzoain, the next village that is 2 km away from the fortress I just escaped. Now, I find myself lost. After several wrong turns, I pull out my guidebook and read what it has to say, "**Lintzoain** - pass pelota court *[F.]* (right) and climb steep narrow defile (recently concreted) into dense mixed woodland. This delightful shaded woodland path continues along a ridge and the *Pasos de Roldán* until we meet."

Going back to the edge of the village, I find my way to the pelota court, which is progress. From here, I'm lost again. I don't know what a "defile" is. I can't see any arrows, and after trying several different routes for quite a distance, I instinctively know they are wrong.

By now, the pink light of dawn has provided enough light to see, and I turn my headlamp off. A few minutes later, I spot two bright ponchos making their way up a narrow street, one I had tried earlier but abandoned for lack of arrows pointing me onwards. Quickly, I catch the walkers in bright ponchos and ask them if this is the way. We don't speak the same language, but it's clear that these ladies are confident of the path. *I guess they know what a defile is.*

After wandering for more than 30 minutes, I'm relieved to be on the right track and have fellow Pilgrims to follow. The path out of Lintzoain is steep. I pass my two Camino angels. They must be walking at a snail's pace, because I pass them with my blazing turtle pace.

In less than an hour, Sheelagh catches up to me. She is poetry in motion, walking sticks and legs working together in smooth forward movement. Watching her closely, I try to copy her movement, the way she holds her sticks and uses them to push forward. I almost fall down from the forward thrust of the sticks. It feels awkward and rushed to walk this way, so I return to my leisurely turtle gait.

Sheelagh seems to enjoy my pace, because she slows down to join me. Sometimes we talk; more often than not, we don't. We each stop to take a picture when we're inspired to do so, enjoying the beauty of the scenery and the newness of our friendship. We are two Pilgrims, sharing the road, walking our own Camino.

We enter Zubiri around 10:30 a.m. and notice there are no Pilgrims to be seen. Our pace has created an unexpected benefit— we continue to walk out of sync with other walkers and have the entire trail and village practically to ourselves.

As we cross the bridge into the village, I am wild to find a bathroom. It's been more than four hours since breaking out of the fortress, and I've been hydrating with water from my platypus, but haven't had a bite to eat.

We locate a "bar" that is serving breakfast. It's the only one that we can see that has any activity at all. Inside, four local men are eating breakfast and smoking. This bar, with its stench of smoke and grease, would not be my first choice to stop for food, but my need to locate indoor plumbing supersedes all others.

Sheelagh is a vegetarian, so her choices are limited. Leaning into this adventure, I order blood sausage and eggs, a dish I had heard about before my trip. Yea, uh, NO. I play with the food to make it appear that I've eaten something, but my stomach is rolling in revolt.

The door to the bathroom is located past the table of four

men. It has a regular door handle that turns (I swear backwards) on a pocket door. To open it, you have to turn and pull sideways. It's so difficult for me to open the bartender/waiter/cook comes out of the kitchen to open it for me.

The lights come on as soon as I enter the bathroom. Carefully, I slide the door closed and turn the lock on the deadbolt. Rushing to the toilet, I give my body a pep talk of encouragement as I remove my belly pack, unbuckle my belt and pull my pants down. Whew, that was close. And then, the lights go out. WHAT? You have got to be kidding me! To activate the motion sensor, I swing my arms wildly, but to no avail. Sitting in the dark, I can hear the voices of the locals through the paper-thin walls and wonder if they can hear me. The bathroom is pitch black, and although I know where all my body parts are located, I need light to gear back up. A crab walk toward the sink activates the light and I'm able to complete my business.

After washing my hands, making sure all my parts are where they need to be, I unlock the door, turn the handle and pull on the door. At least that is what I tried to do, several times, with no success. I can hear laughter through the walls. Twist. Turn. Pull. Nothing. After what feels like an eternity, but is probably only seconds, again the handsome bartender/waiter/cook escorts me through the bathroom door.

The four locals are in full belly-laugh mode now and actually cheer my release, like I had scored a soccer goal. Not knowing what else to do, I raise my arms and yell, "OPA!" I think I channeled *My Big Fat Greek Wedding* and have no idea why. Had I been Greek, maybe, but I am as cracker as they come. The men clap. Sheelagh looks like she's ready to flee, and I'm just glad to be free for the second time in one day. We exit the bar as fast as we can, which isn't very fast.

My breakfast was less than satisfactory, so we make an additional stop at the local grocery store to take some food with us. Our goal is Larrasoaña, or Akerreta, a small village 1 km past Larrasoaña. After each stop, my tendons tighten, and it feels like I'm walking on glass. The first steps after each break are brutal, and my walk is more of a hobble. In time, my tendons stretch out and the pain of the plantar fasciitis subsides.

It is only 6+ km from Zubiri to Larrasoaña, but by the time we arrive at 2:00 p.m., we're wiped out. The trail has been steep and rocky, and we've been walking in a light rain. We have no plans except to get off our feet and take a break. We find a local bar, purchase snacks, hook up to the free WI-FI and enjoy siesta with the locals. It amazes me that while I'm ending my day on the Camino, my husband Gerald's day is just beginning. I wait until after 2:00 p.m. to text Gerald so that I don't wake him up.

The light rain and my sore feet convince Sheelagh and me that we've covered enough ground for the day. My blazing turtle gait was a blinding 1.95 km per hour today. Having made the decision to stay in town, we're tasked with finding a bed for the night. We both prefer sharing a room in a casa rural, pension or hotel over an alburgue. Across from our siesta hangout, we can see the El Perregrino. According to our guidebook, it is a pension. It is right across the street and exactly what we're looking for.

While standing on the porch, waiting for someone to answer the door, we spot an unusual parade of people. In the lead is an American woman radiating the energy of the Pied Piper. She's deep in conversation with a man who appears to be a local and is followed by a large man, whom we assume to be her husband. Our "Buen Camino" is warmly returned and our Pied Piper invites us to join her. She confirms our theory that the man behind her is indeed her husband and they are following the owner of a brand new pension, the San Nicolas, which is less than 60 days old. It's so new that it's not listed in my guidebook.

No one has answered the door yet at El Perregrino, despite multiple attempts. Neither of us knows the proper protocol of bell ringing for service at a pension, so we abandon our current choice to join the parade. When we arrive, we're impressed with the friendliness of the owners and the cleanliness of the building. We ask if we can share a room and sleep on a lower bunk. Receiving an affirmative answer, we make the decision to stay here instead of looking for a semi-private room. After breaking out of a fortress this morning, this modern building is very appealing to me.

We are shown to a tiny room at the top of a steep staircase. The room holds two bunk beds and is located across from the bathroom and shower. Everything is new, modern and clean. Because we have arrived early, we beat the rush for the shower and have time to rest for an entire afternoon.

It doesn't take long for the San Nicolas to fill to capacity. The owner is a good marketer, standing at the bridge as Pilgrims enter the city, enticing them with his warm personality and new construction. A French couple joins our room. The tall, dark haired husband chooses my upper bunk and his petite brunette wife will be sleeping above Sheelagh. They don't speak English and, of course, I don't speak French, but the language of kindness is universal and we're able to communicate our needs without understanding each other's words.

Our room is tiny. With the addition of the French couple, Sheelagh and I head downstairs and sit at one of the many wooden tables in the dining room. There's already an international crowd at our table. Pilgrims from Australia, Ireland, the United States, Netherlands, Holland and Texas are represented. I maintain my states' status as a former country. The room is full of tables and people, and I can see the French couple sitting across the room.

Our early arrival has provided more time to rest today. In addition to my racquetball to work my feet, I bring my "magic stick." The magic stick is basically a round plastic rolling pin that is approximately two feet long, one inch in diameter, with small rollers that melt tension by rolling out the muscles. The magic stick really is magical and it is a gift I can share with my fellow Pilgrims. After demonstrating how to use them, the magic stick and racquetball make the rounds at our table. Justine, the Pied Piper, and her husband, Mike, are the most enthusiastic magic stick users, followed by the Australians. It is, by far, the most enjoyable evening I've experienced on the Camino. With the exception of one, the Pilgrims at our table are laughing, enjoying each other's company and forming friendships that will extend beyond the Camino.

Today has been a day of daring escapes.

Day 5

Stage 3 - Larrasoaña to Pamplona
15 km (9.32 miles)

Last night was uneventful, but loud. Even with earplugs I can hear the Frenchman above me snoring. Or was I hearing myself? It's hard to say. I suspect the other two in our room have suffered the most from our duet.

Sheelagh and I have decided to walk an entire stage from the John Brierley guidebook today. But I'm feeling irritated because it's already 9:30, and we're the only two left in the alburgue. Everyone else has gone. Finally, we're ready to go, backpack swung over my left shoulder, daily pat-down—hat, passport, belly pack, right leg, left leg, let's go. But before we can even step off the porch, the owner, carrying a phone, asks if it belongs to us.

It's not our phone, but it is unlocked. A quick inspection reveals that it belongs to our Pied Piper, Justine. What do we do? Leave it? Or take her phone with us, expecting the Universe to arrange a meeting so that we can return it to her? After a brief discussion on the merits of both plans, we decide to take the phone with us.

Despite my desire to hit the trail, Sheelagh and I cannot pass up the opportunity to take selfies together in front of the Santiago sign. If we don't enjoy ourselves along the way, what's the point?

We cross the bridge that takes us back to the trail and enjoy the outstanding views. As we hike through the forest, I see an attractive wooden sign hanging above our heads advertising a pizza stop in Irotz. It's the first marketing sign I've seen, and the business executive inside me smiles.

Along the way, we take pictures with our phones, and for giggles, we snap a few on Justine's phone. The trail to Irotz is a steep climb on a narrow path. Not anything to fall off of, just single-file walking. It's steep enough for twelve steps and a breath again. In the distance, we see a figure walking towards us, an unusual sight on the Camino. As we near, we see that it's Justine. She's been waiting for us, got impatient and was walking the reverse direction on the Camino. During the time it took Sheelagh and I to walk to Irotz, Mike and Justine have done the same, cabbed back and forth to Larrasoaña, and had time to chill for 90 minutes waiting for us. Geeze, we're slow.

The three of us walk up the hill together. Sheelagh and I drop our packs and poles. I fish out my racquetball for some foot treatment. Mike offers to buy us a tea, and we sit down to swap stories. Although our effort to "help" has delayed their trip, Justine and Mike are gracious and kind.

After our rest, the four of us decide to take the "optional" route to Zabaldica to visit the Church of St. Stephen. The 13th Century church is run by sisters of the Society of the Sacred Heart, and according to our guidebook, allows Pilgrims to climb the bell tower and ring the bell, once.

The directions in our guidebook are unclear, and our beloved yellow arrows are nowhere to be found. Mike stops a local and asks for assistance. Following his instructions, we cross the road and climb a steep hill to the church. As we enter the garden, I see purple bearded iris blooms waving in the breeze. Their presence is a surprise and a boost to my spirit. Although we've seen many flowers along the way and stopped to photograph their beauty, the iris is my favorite flower and a reminder of home.

The nuns provide printed information about the church,

the surrounding area and the Camino, in an amazing variety of languages, organized in a huge rack. After touring the church, we climb the steep, winding, stone staircase to the bell tower. This would be a difficult climb for someone who is claustrophobic. We take turns ringing the bell and enjoy the views from the tower.

Hungry, we pool our resources and enjoy a feast of chocolate, oranges and bread together in the garden. I read the materials provided by the nuns, and I'm moved to my first tears. A tiny nun comes out to greet us. I thank her for the words that touched my soul and we pose for a picture together. The extra kilometers to make this "optional" route are well worth the effort.

Mike will be headed home tomorrow from Pamplona, and Justine will continue her Camino without him. They have reservations tonight in Pamplona at La Perla, a famous five-star hotel frequented by Earnest Hemmingway during his many trips to watch the running of the bulls. The hotel sounds amazing. Sheelagh and I eagerly agree to follow their lead and split the cost of a room. This change of plans means we won't be completing our first stage from the guidebook, but after last night's snore fest, the idea of a luxurious room is too enticing to pass up.

After our feast, Mike and Justine set out for Pamplona at a fast clip. We have made plans to meet for dinner tonight. Sheelagh and I pass through a tunnel and begin the steep climb to Monte Miravavalles, the highest point of our walk today. Here, we're greeted with one of the most beautiful sights and one of the most tragic. In the distance, beautiful fields of cultivated yellow flowers surround the city, yet we pass graffiti-blemished walls that surround an electric plant. The contrast between nature's handiwork versus human handiwork could not be starker.

We pass over an ancient bridge and quickly step into another world. Like St. Jean, buildings rise above our heads on both sides, and we enter a canyon of humanity that seems to stretch on forever. According to my guidebook, Pamplona has a population of 200,000, and on this Sunday, it feels like most of the people are on the street. Families shepherd small children and soccer balls. Dogs walking their owners. Groups of friends gather at outdoor cafés, drinking, eating, smoking, laughing and talking. After the quiet of the Camino, my ears feel assaulted.

We stop for a bathroom break and foot massage in one of the many squares. Sheelagh is reunited with a fellow Irishman whom she met in Orrison. At home, I would never consider removing my shoes in a café, but here on the Camino it is standard practice.

Before my trip, I thought "ancient roadways" sounded romantic. Cobblestone is in fact the hardest surface for my poor knees and feet to endure, and we have 4 km of concrete and cobblestone to cross before we reach our hotel.

Coming into the historic center of Pamplona is quite exciting. We pass over a drawbridge and enter through a stone gate. It is our first big city to navigate, and unfortunately neither of us can find our way to the hotel. Despite our map-reading deficiency, I am thankful for the companionship of my witty Irish Camino angel. We ask a policeman for directions and he points across the square to our hotel. *Aack*, at least we're close.

We check into the hotel and I'm handed the fanciest key I've ever seen in my life. The key is attached to a giant maroon tassel and feels like it weighs at least a half-pound. We refuse the porter's offer to carry our backpacks. Even if we're checking into a five-star hotel, we're still Pilgrims and can carry our stuff.

After shepherding us into our room, the bellman opens the windows overlooking a narrow street and shows us the directions that the bulls run. Leaning out, I can imagine Hemmingway doing the same.

Our room is sleek and modern. Expecting a bathtub in a luxurious hotel, I'm disappointed to find a shower large enough for an entire basketball team. "Why couldn't they have left a tub and made the shower smaller?"

And then I laugh. Expectations, when not met, cause disappointment. Here I am in a beautiful comfortable room, with a delightful new friend and I'm feeling disappointed? I don't think so. Smiling, I slip back into gratitude. Keeping an open mind to the unfolding of life is one of the keys to happiness.

Using WhatsApp, we communicate a time and place to meet Mike and Justine. But our room is so comfortable that neither Sheelagh nor I are motivated to leave. We wait until the very last second to leave and hurry to the café, but we're too late. Mike and

Justine have just left. We look up and down the street but can't locate them.

I feel terrible that they waited on me twice today. In my heart, I know that everything always works out for our highest good and suspect that Mike and Justine will have a great last night together without the two of us tagging along. But I also resolve to be more careful about what I am willing to do, or not do, with my time and not keep others waiting.

Pamplona offers a wide variety of places to eat. Sheelagh and I wander café to café. Between Sheelagh's vegetarian need and my pickiness, coming to agreement is difficult.

In a bar/café, we see a group of Pilgrims we know and decide to join them. Despite my earlier vow to be more careful with my time, I find myself joining the group to attend mass, even though I really don't want to go. I'm pretty sure Sheelagh feels the same.

The craftsmanship of the cathedral is amazing, yet I can't help but feel uncomfortable with the opulence and sacrifices made by ordinary people to pay for it. Rather than receive any kind of peace from the sermon, my discomfort grows. It's not the language barrier, it's me. I feel closer to God in the midst of Nature than I do inside this manmade temple. When everyone stands, I make the decision to jet. Sheelagh is right on my heels.

Relieved to be free, we resume our search for a good meal. We find a restaurant and are seated in a back room. Twenty minutes later, the group of Pilgrims that we had left at mass enter the restaurant. They are seated a few tables away and are as surprised as we are to see each other. Such is the way of the Camino.

Returning to our room, we connect to Wi-Fi and check out our new Camino friends on Facebook. We discover that Andrea, our Italian selfie-stick friend from the fortress is somewhere in Pamplona tonight too. Wonder what happened? At the pace he travels he should be days ahead of us. Our earlier posts have drawn comments from our Australian friends from last night.

They are poking fun at us for staying at La Perla.

The comments left on my Facebook page were expected. By posting my stay at La Perla, sharing my Camino of Ease and Grace, I received comments of judgment and criticism, which is fine. It opens up the dialogue that the Camino can be enjoyed however you are called to experience it. Living in fear of what others say or think is living life small, and does not lead to happiness.

La Perla Hotel has the nicest European bathroom I have used yet on the Camino, and it is unlikely that I will see another like it anytime soon. Rather than wait a full week from my departure to clean and treat the hole in my gum, I am taking advantage of this spacious, modern, brightly lit, clean bathroom to face this unpleasant task. I have no experience in completing this procedure and am not looking forward to it. Gulp.

Without going into gory details, I'm happy to report that all went well. The flap cover is back in place. The gum is healing nicely, and with this first success behind me, I am confident that next time will be even easier. I repack the bottle of Paradox, 10X mirror, plastic dental syringe, and ultra-soft toothbrush in its special bag and put it in the bottom of my backpack.

Sheelagh has decided to mail a package home tomorrow morning to lighten her load. I ask myself, *What can I do without?*

Day 6

Stages 3 & 4 - Pamplona to Puente la Reina
24.2 km (15.04 miles)

Since it is Monday, Sheelagh is able to mail her package home. We know from experience that she will catch me on the trail. It's 9:30 a.m. before we leave, Sheelagh to find the post office, and me to find the Camino path in the busy city. My first turn puts me going the wrong way on the Camino. It's not until I see Pilgrims walking towards me that I realize I'm not heading in the right direction. The good news is that I haven't gone far. Before leaving town, I purchase a snack for my pack. The map shows several long sections between available stops today, and I feel more comfortable carrying some food for fuel on these long stretches.

The beautiful fields of yellow flowers return on the other side of Pamplona. The concrete path gives way to the steep, natural path leading to the wind turbines. It's a scene straight from *The Way*, one I've been looking forward to experiencing in person. At 12:30, I stop at a bench between Cruce and Zariquiegui to eat my breakfast, stretch my feet and enjoy the view. Many Pilgrims pass me, some I've seen before and others who are new faces. It doesn't take long to spot the familiar Irish blonde coming up the trail followed by Andrea, our Italian friend. The three of us share stories and laughter until Andrea hurries off.

Sheelagh and I follow at our usual slow pace. We stop in Zariquiegui for a much needed bathroom break. The next opportunity is more than 6 km away, on the other side of the mountain. I'm ready to leave but Sheelagh is enjoying the break. Rather than wait for her, always knowing that she will catch up, I leave on my own, happy for solitude up the Alto de Perdon, or Hill of Forgiveness. My mind is full of people I have yet to forgive, including myself.

Reaching the top is not easy. The path is rugged and challenging, which makes it more fun for me. I would not want to walk the entire Camino this way, but for this section the added challenge makes this Hill of Forgiveness more real. Each struggling, stumbling step up is an opportunity to forgive.

Nearing the top, I am thrilled to be this close to the wind turbines and stop to video the sound. The sounds of the Camino are as enchanting as the views, but more difficult to capture. My earlier attempts to catch the gentle breeze blowing through the trees sound like whistling wind on the phone. The turbine video is moderately successful. I can hear the slicing of the blades through the air over the wind noise.

Rather than rush the moment, I enjoy the views of Pamplona from the bench at the top of the hill. I can even see the path we walked yesterday coming into Pamplona.

Stopping makes my feet hurt, so I don't sit for long. Trudging up and over the top, I can see the Peregrino Monument and feel like I'm on a movie set. Another couple has reached the top and we take turns photographing each other. This is a legacy moment in my life. A time to hit the pause button and soak it in, to remember later. I can feel the presence of those who have come before me and relish sharing their energy.

And then, there is the food truck. They didn't show that in the movie, or talk about it in my guidebook. It's quite unexpected and makes me feel sad. And then, it hits me. It's not the presence of the food truck that has caused my sadness; it is another example of unmet expectations. The food truck does not match the movie in my head. Realizing the cause of my unhappiness lets me release the sadness, and I continue on my way with a smile on my face. Thank you, food truck, for the reminder lesson.

The guidebook's symbol for caution is an exclamation point inside a red oval. Today's map shows the caution symbol on the next section of my trail, the downhill side of this mountain. Since I was able to recapture my happiness, and capture the energy of prior Pilgrims, this downhill walk is fun. The perfect weather helps. I shudder to think what it would be like to walk this in the rain. The trail is so steep that wooden beams have been placed across the path to reduce erosion. It reminds me of the hike down the Grand Canyon I made a few years ago with Gerald and his cousins. I say a prayer of gratitude for the Ease and Grace I'm experiencing on my journey.

Sheelagh catches me before I reach the bottom of the hill. We swap stories of our experience on the hill and discuss alternatives for tonight's lodging. We enjoy each other's company and appreciate the opportunity to split the cost of semi-private quarters. It's 4:00 p.m. when we reach Uterga, and Sheelagh is done for the day. We're standing in front of a lovely private alburgue and take our picture in front of the "Santiago 697 km" sign. Unbelievably, I have more life in my legs and feet and am not ready to stop yet. I am being pulled forward and honor the pull.

Two hours later, I hobble into Puente la Reina, exhausted. The Alburgue Jakue is waiting for me at the head of the trail. The hospitalera can see my exhaustion and shows me to my bunk through a maze of corridors. The building is actually a hotel and alburgue combined. The alburgue side is quite large and has several rooms of bunks sectioned off by screens. The hospitalera shows me to a section next to the women's shower room, and I am the only occupant in this section. Entering the shower, I can see why they've provided separate showers for men and women. Inside the women's shower room are three very modern, clear-glass shower pods with a rain head and a bank of massage heads. This bathroom would be challenging for a modest person. Modest or not, washing your privates in public is no fun. For me, it isn't a problem because I'm the only one in the shower room. I say another prayer of gratitude for the Ease and Grace I've enjoyed.

This alburgue offers one of the most unusual Pilgrim meals on the Camino; it is served buffet style. After stuffing my laundry in a machine to wash, I wear my pajamas to dinner. The dining room is quite large, the food buffet set up in the first room and dining tables in an adjoining room. Scanning the room for a table, I see a man sitting by himself. I'm drawn to his table and ask him if he would like company for dinner. He smiles and assures me he has been waiting for the right person to join him. And without knowing why, I recognize that I was called forward today to share this meal with this man.

His name is Dennis, a fellow American. He is seventy-plus-years young, but doesn't look it. We discover commonality after commonality. I feel like I'm having dinner with an old friend. He is walking his second Camino and his approach is the polar opposite of mine. It is fascinating to hear how he planned his Camino.

Dennis spent months preparing for this journey, drawing on experiences from his previous Camino. He knows exactly how far he will walk each day and has reservations for a private room each night. His guidebook is different from mine and more conducive for shorter walks each day. He has written his hotel information in a little black book and generously shares the information with me. In the middle of our conversation, I limp back to the washing machine to move my laundry to the dryer. When I return, we resume our conversation and finish our Pilgrim wine. Pilgrim meals come with water or wine; tonight, we drink wine. Dennis is from California, so he is a connoisseur of wine. I'm hoping it will dull the pain in my feet.

After dinner, we make our way down the stairs and to the lodging side of the building. Dennis' room is across from the laundry, and I peek inside to see what a private room in an alburgue looks like. Nice. My clothes are sitting on top of the dryer and have already been neatly folded. We say "Buen Camino" and then I squirrel my way to the alburgue side of the building to nestle in my bunk. I am lulled to sleep by the coughs, snores and farts of my fellow Pilgrims. Meeting Dennis has rocked my world tonight. I can't wait to tell Sheelagh what I have learned.

I'm not sure exactly, but I do know something changed today. Not only did I walk an entire stage from my guidebook, I walked extra kilometers from the day before. Somehow I managed to walk 24.5 km and meet Dennis. Was it the Pilgrim energy I tapped into, or did something shift on the Hill of Forgiveness?

Day 7

Stage 5 - Puente la Reina to Estella
21.9 km (13.6 miles)

This morning my throat is a bit sore, so my first stop will be to find hot water for an Emergen-C® with breakfast. It is 7:45 and my goal for the day is to make it to Estella, 21.9 km away. With yesterday's success, I'm feeling confident I can make another stage walk from my guidebook. The day feels different. I'm comfortable walking alone, enjoying the solitude of the day and content with my own company.

I enjoy my solitude and am unafraid when I see a man walking towards me. He is obviously a local because he doesn't carry a backpack and is dressed in regular clothes. The energy he's sending is one of kindness, respect and curiosity. I stand aside at the top of steep steps to allow him to pass, and to rest for a moment. When he reaches the top, he smiles, offers the standard "Buen Camino" greeting and gestures for me to proceed down the stairs. And then, he reverses his course, follows me down and joins me on the trail. Although our ability to speak each other's language is quite limited, we're able to converse. He understands I'm a Texan walking the Camino alone, and I understand he's taking his daily walk in the beautiful countryside. Reaching the town's edge, we say goodbye with a hug and a kiss-kiss on the cheeks, celebrating the connection we shared, and then continue on our separate ways.

Just past Cirauqui my pack begins to feel extremely heavy, like gravity is pulling it down. My friend, Yvonne, has warned me about this phenomenon, but this is the first time I've felt it. According to Yvonne, the original Camino followed the ley lines of the Earth, and when the route deviates off of them, the pack will feel heavy. Looking at the map, this section of the trail deviates away from the road that was built next to the original Camino. I have no idea if what she says is true, but it does explain the sudden difference.

My heavy pack reminds me of my conversation with Dennis last night. He said, "We pack our fears in our backpack." If that is true, and I think it is, I can see that I'm afraid to be wet and cold. I'm carrying rain pants, rain coat, gloves, scarf, poncho and backpack cover to protect me from the rain. But I think it is deeper than that. I am carrying a rock that I brought from home that represents the limiting beliefs and stories that no longer serve me. I will leave the rock at Cruz de Ferro on Stage 24. It's a long way from here and the rock weighs heavy on my heart.

By noon, I've made it to the Rio Saldo and cross its medieval bridge. The bank is flat and provides easy access to cool waters to soak my feet. I am not alone; many Pilgrims have stopped to enjoy the river and eat. I'm the only one with my feet in the water. Looking up, I see Dennis crossing the bridge. I wave but he doesn't see me. He is in his walking zone.

Feeling refreshed from the cold water, I begin the second half of my journey to Estella. In Lorca, I see Lou, a Canadian I met in Hunto at breakfast on Day 1. He's sitting in a chair, suffering from blisters. He tells me he plans to stay here for the night. He seems fascinated that I've made it this far and voices his astonishment in my accomplishment. Lou has made the mistake of judging me by my looks instead of my heart. I wish him "Buen Camino" and shuffle onwards with a big smile on my face.

Just past Lorca, I meet Juanetta, an Australian woman walking alone. Her Camino story is very unusual. While she walks each day, her husband enjoys the countryside on a rented motorcycle. They meet up at the end of the day and stay in a hotel. Because he is not a Pilgrim, they are staying in hotels along the way.

Juanetta and I fall into a shared rhythm of walking and enjoy each other's company. We explore the differences and similarities between our countries as well as our Camino experience. She mentions the unusual feeling of a heavy backpack today that coincides with my experience. I think Yvonne was right about the ley lines.

As Juanetta and I enter the small town of Villatuerta, my bladder is whispering, "Hey girl, give me a break." Unfortunately, it's siesta time and everything is closed." I know because I try every door of any establishment that looks like a café, alburgue or bar.

We continue on. The closer we get to Estella, the more my body is in conflict. My bladder is screaming at me to hurry, but my feet are refusing to obey. My feet hurt so bad, my pace has slowed back to turtle gait. The final 4 km is spent reminding my bladder of our commitment to indoor plumbing. Juanetta, God love her, stays with me until we reach our destination, then we part ways.

Alone again, my feet win the battle of my body. I must rest them for a moment before I find a bathroom. Standing, my feet on fire, I lurch forward. I hear the sound of laughter to my right and see my Pied Piper friend, Justine, surrounded by Pilgrims enjoying a glass of wine in front of a bar. She introduces me to her companions as her Camino angel and tells the story of her phone. She invites me to join them which gives me the opportunity to leave my pack and use the facilities. When I return, Justine invites me to join her and this fun group at the municipal alburgue across from the bar. Thanking her, I decline. I'm determined to locate the hotel written in Dennis' black book. The idea of sleeping alone, in quiet solitude, sounds divine.

Leaving Justine and her merry band of Pilgrims behind, I lumber on to find El Volante Hotel. As I'm gimping through town, a young man stops me and asks if I've found a place to stay for the night. He suggests the new alburgue at the monastery, just up the road. I thank him for the information, but I'm committed to my privacy tonight. The map shows El Volante is on the far side of town. When I arrive at the spot on the map, I cannot find the hotel. Instead, I find a bar by the same name. The waiter points me to an unmarked doorway across the street. Hobbling back across the street, I haul myself up the stairs and discover the door is locked. I see an intercom button, but I'm too intimidated to push it. Instead, I reverse course and backtrack to the monastery I passed on the way, the one the young man recommended. I *trust* the Universe has better plans for me and I surrender to the flow. My feet are threatening mutiny. It is all I can do to make it to my room on the second floor.

Entering the room, I see two bunk beds and one woman. Tanja, from Germany, is sitting on the bottom bunk near the window. The other bottom bunk is covered in Pilgrim paraphernalia. It doesn't take a rocket scientist to figure out I have my choice of upper bunks tonight. Yikes.

The small room has a lived in feel to it. Tanja gathers her things to give me room to put my backpack down. She has been here for several days, recovering from a leg injury and has stuff spread everywhere. As I unpack, I offer her the magic stick and show her how to use it, then I leave for the bathroom.

A hot shower helps. By the time I return to the room, it's empty, and I utilize the opportunity to relax by myself. My feet refuse to budge. Rather than go out for dinner, I scrounge in my pack, find a partial loaf of stale bread, an orange and a chocolate bar to eat. It's enough to satisfy my hunger. The door opens as I finish my dinner and, to my surprise, Louise, my Canadian taxi-sharing friend from St. Jean, steps into the room. She is my bottom bunkmate tonight. We catch up on our paths that have brought us back together. Her daughter, Ashley, is ahead of her, traveling at her own pace. Louise has slowed down and is nursing a leg injury.

She invites me to dinner and to explore the town. Thanking her for the invitation, I decline and enjoy my solitude. Hauling myself up to the top bunk is not pretty, and I'm glad that no one is here to see me. I just want to get horizontal and rest my feet.

I must have fallen asleep because I wake up when Louise and Tanja return from dinner. Clumsily, I crawl down from my bunk and make one last trip to the bathroom to brush my teeth, put in my mouth guard and empty my bladder. Shuffling back to the room, I plead with my body to cooperate tonight. I don't want to climb up and down in the dark for a midnight run to the bathroom.

I'm normally a restless sleeper, flopping like a fish out of water. My goal is to lie still all night and not flop out of the top bunk. I've never worried about falling out of a bunk before now, but I've never slept this high before. As I lay in the darkness, holding still, I have a tiny taste of what my brother Richard must be going through. He has been sleeping on an upper bunk in a federal prison for almost 18 months now.

His prison sentence has been a shock to our entire family. Richard is an All-American football player, a nice guy and an honorable man. He is the first in our family to be convicted of any crime. My best resource to help me through this situation has been to GRIPP Life.

Empathy is the ability to understand and share another person's experiences and emotions. Tonight, from this upper bunk, I am given the gift of empathy for my brother's experience. I am grateful to the Universe for this opportunity to peek into Richard's world.

Day 8

※

Stage 6 - Estella to Los Arcos
21.4 km (13.3 miles)

The day is already a roaring success. I made it through the night without flopping out of bed or making a midnight run to the bathroom. Climbing out of bed this morning is easier, because Tanja pushes a chair to me to use as a stepstool. So much easier than struggling with the tiny steps mounted to the side of the bed. I am surprised at how good I feel. The body's ability to restore itself each night is truly a miracle.

Breakfast service ends at 8:00 and is included in the 15 euros I paid last night for my bed. The offering includes hot chocolate, a cookie-like biscuit and 2 rolls. I save the rolls for later and am ready to hit the trail by 8:45. My goal today is Los Arcos, 21.4 km away, another full stage from my guidebook. Louise joins me this morning. We're looking forward to drinking wine from the famous Estella wine font.

There are water fonts all along the Camino that provide free fresh spring water. The Estella font is the only one offering wine. Our water system at home is a rain water catchment, so I'm comfortable drinking from the fonts. According to Gerald, I'm a water snob, and he's right. My taste buds are powerful funk detectors, and so far, the water has been fantastic. Each day, I check the location of fonts in my guidebook. If there is only one, I fill my platypus to its 3-liter capacity, adding more than 7 pounds of weight to my pack. If there are several fonts available, I partially fill it to save weight.

Just as Louise and I trudge past the turnoff to the Voltaire Hotel, Dennis pops around the corner. Laughing at the serendipity of our meeting, we enjoy catching up from our dinner two nights ago. Drinking wine at 8:30 in the morning is not my norm, but it is a tradition on the Camino to take a sip from the Estella wine font. We join the jovial crowd that has gathered to partake in this ritual. The sounds of laughter and the clicks of cameras fill the air. The wine's flavor? Well, let's just say there's a reason that it's free.

Louise is enjoying the moment, but Dennis and I are ready to go. First we review the map to choose which path we will take. Each day there are multiple routes to choose from. Today's choice is the high road or the low road. From reading my Australian friend's Facebook page, I know the rugged high road route offers amazing views of remote countryside. For me, the low road is my preferred route because it offers occasional stops along the way for breaks. Dennis agrees, and we follow the path to Monjardin, enjoying the sounds of the birds and the beauty of the pine forest.

By the time we reach Azqueta, we're both ready for a second breakfast. The food is delicious and the outdoor café is conducive for attending to our feet. Dennis changes socks and I roll my feet on my ball and stretch the tendons in my leg. Another Pilgrim is massaging her legs, so I offer her the use of the Magic Stick, which elicits moans and smiles.

After our breakfast, Dennis takes the lead, with his earbuds pumping music. I prefer to listen to the birds, the wind and the sound of my feet crunching on the path. My iPod is stored deep within my backpack, waiting for the Meseta. According to my research, the Meseta is a long, flat boring walk after we reach Burgos that continues for more than a week. It's hard for me to imagine anything being boring on this journey, but just in case, I'm saving my music to keep me company when and if it happens.

The day is a blur of green pastures, occasional fields of yellow flowers, distant mountains and puffy clouds spitting occasional rain on us. My favorite sight is watching the wind blow the grass, like waves, creating a sea of green. The gravel path takes us past a marker topped with flowers planted in a worn out boot and magnificent bushes covered in purple flowers.

The map shows no cafés, villages or available services for the final 8.8 km into Los Arcos, so I'm surprised to see a concession stand surrounded by six tables and chairs, offering snacks and drinks. We agree to take advantage of this unexpected gift to take care of our feet and enjoy a glass of fresh-squeezed orange juice. It is now my official favorite drink. I'm beginning to understand Sue's comment about the obsession with feet, and I'm cognizant of my change in attitude for this concession stand as compared to the food truck at the top of the Hill of Forgiveness.

Each day, you never know who you will see on the trail. Today, I have seen Juanetta, my Australian companion from yesterday, the two ladies who helped me when I was lost on Day 3, and an adorable Korean couple whose path I have crossed often and whose pace matches my own. Together, the three of us have been passed by many Pilgrims as we've struggled up and down several mountain paths. The Korean man is covered from head to toe, protecting the light color of his skin and his place in his culture. His companion is protected, but does not cover her face, sharing her smile with all who pass. Each chance encounter is cherished.

At the Los Arcos sign, I convince Dennis to take a selfie with me in celebration of our arrival. It is a big deal for me. Walking with Dennis today, my pace has picked up to a blazing 3.3 km per hour. The Camino leads us through the center of town, and I'm intrigued by the signs of new construction. Modern houses butt next to ancient stone structures. Barricades protect newly laid stone streets, and children run past, shooting each other with squirt guns.

Feeling like a stalker, I follow Dennis to his hotel, hoping for a room, despite my lack of reservation. Hostel Ezequiel is not located on the Camino, but it isn't difficult to get to either. I am in luck, and by 3:45, I am in bliss. A bed to myself, with ample time to shower, take care of my feet, do laundry, catch up with Gerald, post on Facebook and send Richard an email before meeting Dennis for dinner. Earlier I saw other Pilgrims check in to the hotel, but the restaurant is empty at 7:00. Strange. Dennis and I have the entire restaurant to ourselves. Our three-course Pilgrim meal tonight includes beans, chicken, chocolate ice cream and wine.

Today marks the beginning of my second week of the journey, and memories from the past week flood my mind. The joys and the tragedies. I wonder, does getting in bed with a French woman and flooding the floor count as a tragedy? I recall many moments of pain, and the ability to push through it. But most of all, the memory of trudging over the Pyrenees Mountains in the snow, facing the horrific wind and driving rain, and proclaiming it "the best day ever!"

Before the Camino, one of my daily reminders was "Each day is a gift." But now, in less than a week, saying "Best day ever!" has more meaning, which is amazing to me. "Each day is a gift" is etched on the center of my parents' joint headstone.

When Dad was diagnosed with lung cancer, he began pre-planning his funeral, with the expectation of beating the odds. During one of the good days between radiation treatments, when he was particularly optimistic about getting better, we talked about his plans. Two days later, he fell, broke his hip, and his cancer treatments were suspended. It was the beginning of a very quick end.

After his death, I discovered paperwork in which he

negotiated a discount for his own funeral and approved the custom engraving of his tombstone. The words are etched in his handwriting. Mixed in with the papers was a birthday card I had given him. I had signed the card with "Each day is a gift." I am grateful he kept the card for me to find and to realize the impact my words had on him.

"Best day ever" has spontaneously emerged as my mantra for this journey. Although my intention was to walk the Camino with Ease and Grace, I had no idea what that meant before I left. In just a week, I already understand that it is a mini-course for life. I'm learning to live the best day ever, no matter how bad my feet hurt, how hungry I get, or how many upper bunks I sleep in.

I am trusting my intuition more and acting on it quicker. And with Dennis' help, I am more genuine and courageous in enjoying this journey with Ease and Grace. He has reminded me that I don't have to walk a stage a day and that I can enjoy my privacy.

Tomorrow, I have given myself permission to deviate from the guidebook's 28.6 km stage to Logroño. Instead, an 18.6 km hike to Viana feels better. *And* I made reservations for a night at the Palacio de Pujadas. Thank you, dear Camino Angel, Dennis.

Email to Richard:

I made it another stage today. From Estella to Los Arcos . . . Last night I stayed at an alburgue on the top bunk. I thought of you . . . My feet, knees and back are holding up pretty well. I stop along the way and take care of them.

More later,
I love you

Day 9

Stage 7 - Los Arcos to Viana
18.6 km (11.56 miles)

This morning, I navigate my way to the square and find a café for a quick bite before hitting the trail. Expecting it to warm up today, I'm layered in my green shirt for cool days over my white shirt for warm days. Their combined warmth is enough for the early morning coolness and provides easy adjustment later on to stay comfortable in changing temperatures throughout the day.

As I near the edge of town, I see a group of large, carved stone artwork and stop to capture their unusual and striking beauty. The path this morning is concrete, crowded by houses on both sides. I'm climbing, but gently. As I climb, the houses give way to orchards and occasional homes with fenced yards occupied by small packs of big shaggy dogs, who ignore the ongoing parade of Pilgrims passing by. At the top of the rise, I stop and turn around. A single church spire rises above the city, backlit by the dawn, reaching upwards to touch the golden sky. Looking backwards is powerful. From this higher ground, I can appreciate the pain and struggle it took for me to arrive at this place of beauty.

The path continues to climb through fenced agriculture fields. I'm confused by several large, chipped, ceramic insulators sitting next to fence posts, until I come over another rise and see the electric substation. With my construction and real estate background, I'm fascinated by Spain's infrastructure in the midst of the natural beauty of the landscape.

According to my map, there are only two stops today between Los Arcos and Viana. Sansol, the first stop, is sitting at the crest of today's first peak. Although it is only 3.8 km from my starting point, I gladly take a seat at the first café I find. Before I can finish my foot treatment and snack, I am joined by Sheelagh. Dear, Sheelagh! I am overjoyed to see her again and amazed to learn that she had to work hard to catch me. She spotted my signature pink crocs, swinging from my backpack, and had been trying to catch me for several kilometers. The body adapts quickly. My lung capacity has improved, which has given me the ability to walk uphill without stopping every twelve steps. Although it has only been three days since we've seen each other, it feels like a lifetime. Our hearts have come to an unspoken agreement to walk together again today. Rather than hurry, I wait for her to eat her snack and enjoy hearing the tales of her adventures. I am laughing to the point of tears.

At our next foot stop, Rio Cornava, I see Juanetta coming towards us. Sheelagh and Juanetta haven't met yet, so I introduce them. We come from Ireland, Texas and Australia, but it feels more like we're sisters. The three of us continue together and reach Viana before 2:00. My pace is a satisfying 3.1 km per hour today.

After enjoying a cold beer with us, Juanetta sets off for Logroño to meet her motorcycle-riding husband. Sheelagh and I order lunch from our outdoor café table. The café is directly on the Camino route, across from another beautiful church. The bells ring loud and often during the time we enjoy our front-row seat to Pilgrims traipsing by.

First up is the lovely French couple we slept with in Larrasoaña. Our foursome is back together and the joy of seeing each other is mutual. Although we lack the ability to understand each other's language, we speak Camino: the language of the heart. Nowhere else can you spend the night with a stranger, listen to them snore all night and still be ecstatic to see them in the future. Before they head off, we share hugs, selfies and laughter.

Our meal is interrupted several times to hug, wave or "Buen Camino" friends and Pilgrims who look like they could use some encouragement to continue. On the Camino, everyone is either a friend, or a friend who you haven't met yet.

We watch as a group of parents congregate in the square next to the church and wonder what is happening. The parents start to cheer, so we stand to get a better glimpse of what the commotion is about. Coming towards us is a real parade of middle-school children dressed in *Alice in Wonderland* costumes. Today is book day, and the children are celebrating with a parade to honor this classic story.

Three boys approach our table, and I'm gifted a poem, tied as a scroll with a piece of yarn. Gratitude for this day washes over me. The decision to stay in Viana has provided more than I could ever have dreamed, and the day is not done.

Sheelagh has decided to book her own room at the Pujadas tonight. After the parade breaks up, we check into the hotel. The room is outstanding and I fall asleep in the bathtub. Waking up, I make it to the bed for an official nap. We meet before dinner to explore the city, which doesn't take long because of its quaint size.

We discover a gorgeous but horrifically damaged church, and I wonder what century the damage occurred. On the other side of the church is a plaza. A mix of locals and Pilgrims are lounging in the grass, catching the last rays of the setting sun, or leaning over the wall to enjoy the long-distance views of the valley below. The energy is relaxed and peaceful.

As we stroll past a trio of local boys—they look fourteen or so—one stops me to ask, "Excuse me, is your hair natural? It is so sexy!" With a giggle on the inside, I assure the young man, that yes, indeed, my snow-white hair is natural. My white hair began showing up in my mid-thirties, thanks to the DNA passed to me from my maternal great-grandmother. But it wasn't until my mother passed away that it was allowed to shine. There was no way in hell that my mother would tolerate her only daughter to go grey before her. My wise friend, Art, explains it this way, "You know why Texas women don't go grey? Because grandma is still dyeing her hair."

In fading light, Sheelagh and I begin our search for a place to eat dinner. We pass through the injured church where moonlight streams through a hole in the ceiling. Most Spanish restaurants do not open until eight o'clock, but on the Camino, many offer a Pilgrim meal that begins at seven. Wandering through town, we fail to find a restaurant that passes both our tests: Sheelagh's vegetarian menu and my intuitive guide. There are several that offer vegetarian food, but my inner guide warns me away. In the end, we return to our lunch café and enjoy a non-pilgrim meal of paella and mushroom risotto.

On the way back to the hotel, we discover a cozy tearoom run by an American couple. We eat a delicious slice of carrot cake and sip a warm cup of tea, while warming our feet next to the small gas fireplace. Soft, soothing music plays in the background. What a wonderful way to live the best day ever!

Leaving the tea room, we hear the sound of clapping, setting the tempo for a live orchestra playing above our heads. The sign on the building says *Casa de Cultura*. We pause and enjoy the sound of their music before returning to our hotel.

The bonus of having a room to myself is that I get to sleep naked. In doing so, I see that I have a bizarre Pilgrim tan that includes my fingers and half of my hands. Between my hat, long sleeves and pants, everything else is protected from the sun. As I lay in bed, remembering the day, I smile. Viana is my favorite city yet.

Day 10

Stages 7 & 8 - Viana to Navarette
22.7 km (14.1 miles)

Bizarre dreams of killing people last night woke me up more than once. This is a first. One that I am attributing to the history of the area, or this building. Usually I don't remember my dreams, and when I do they are weird in quirky ways: like floating against the flow in a canoe on the stream behind my childhood home, passing yawning hippopotamuses. But never killing people.

Sheelagh and I enjoy breakfast together. After breakfast, I'm ready to go, but Sheelagh isn't, so we agree to meet in Navarette tonight. Before leaving, I ask the woman at the front desk to make a reservation at a pension for Sheelagh and me to share a room tonight. Pensions are a step above alburgues and hostels. Unfortunately the woman is unable to get through; the phone lines aren't working. Having tried to plan, I'm content to let the day unfold.

Leaving the hotel, I see Louise and her American friend Laura. They're eating breakfast in the restaurant of our hotel. After a quick catch up, a hug and Buen Camino, I'm off. It's somewhere between 8:15 and 8:30.

On my way out of town, I see an array of parents walking their children to school. A Muslim woman, wrapped in her burqa, is pushing a stroller with her school-aged child walking dutifully next to the stroller. An attentive father, holding his kindergarten-size daughter's hand, hanging on to her every word, turns toward the school in front of me as I pass.

The route leaving Viana is a gentle downhill slope, and although I've been walking for quite some time, already deep into the agriculture fields that surround the city, I suddenly hear music blasted from speakers. The music is beautiful, so I stop to record it on my phone as a video. I assume it's the *Spanish National Anthem* coming from the school I passed on my way out of town.

My next destination is Logroño. According to the guidebook, Logroño has a population of 155,000 people, almost as big as Pamplona. It's also the first city in the region of La Rioja, so named for its rich red dirt, which is excellent for growing grapes. Nearing the city, I see from the map that I will be crossing the N-111 for the seventh time since leaving Los Arcos yesterday. But this time is different. This time I climb eighteen stairs to the elevated bridge to reach the other side. Stopping in the middle, I watch the traffic rush under me and marvel at the dedication of resources that supports modern day Pilgrims.

After crossing the N-111 again, I begin to see signs of civilization. My solitude is shattered by a large parade of school children headed my way. There are so many of them, they clog the entire route. As I weave my way through them, I feel like a salmon swimming upstream.

Once the parade passes, I'm on my own again. The path under my feet has changed to a beautiful smooth brick pathway, lined on both sides by tall evergreens that I call cemetery trees, because in Texas that is where you find most of them.

As I near the Rio Ebro, I see my first stork perched on top of its nest on a manmade electric line tower. I pause to take a picture. To me, the storks sound like those wind-up fake teeth chattering on a table. Moving on, my first view of the bridge crossing the river is breathtaking. The stairs leading to the bridge are worthy of taking a photo. So is the scene of the river from the center of the bridge. The contrast of modern cars parked on the ancient streets of Logroño deserves to be captured as well.

What in the world is happening to me? I wonder as I snap photo after photo. This causes me to reflect back. I was an avid photographer at one time, even going so far as to purchase professional equipment to pursue a sports photography career when my girls were playing volleyball in high school. But after my parents passed away, and I was faced with going through their mountains of photographs, my desire to take any picture trickled to almost zero.

It was heartbreaking to go through their photographs and decide which ones to keep, share or throw away. As the only daughter, the task fell to me to sort and decide, a project that remains ongoing. Photographs of my parents growing up, mostly of mom since her father was an amateur photographer. My father grew up poor so there were very few childhood photos of him. Photographs of me and my brothers growing up, and the trips we took as a family. Photographs of my parents' nine grandchildren, at every stage of life, baby pictures, school pictures, birthday pictures, first dance pictures, holiday pictures, sports pictures and family pictures. Boxes and boxes of just scenery, taken who knows where from their many trips around the world, were mixed with photos of their friends in exotic places. And then, there were videos, from 8 mm to VCR, and everything in between.

In the subsequent years since their passing, Gerald and I have made a first and second pass of going through our boxes of pictures and giving them away, while we're alive. We intend to "tidy up" before we go. From the quizzical look on our children's faces, when we hand them another box of pictures, I know they don't understand. I gladly accept their irritation now in exchange for sparing them the heartbreak of sorting through boxes of photos, blinded by tears, after I'm gone.

The recent addition of grandchildren in my life increased

my appreciation for pictures again. But today's picture taking craze is new, born from embracing my authenticity and increased stamina. The photos capture the memories of my Camino, but without the story behind the photos, they become just another box of pictures. As I look at all the sites that Logroño has to offer, I wonder what wonderful memories my parents created in the mountains of photos they collected during their life. Stories that are lost forever. Telling the story behind the photo takes time, but it is imperative. Without the story behind the photos, the legacy is lost.

Getting through Logroño is easier than expected, until I hit construction. And even then, the short stray off the path isn't difficult because a kind woman escorts me back to the Camino. I was lost and didn't even know it. Big yellow arrows, installed on the sidewalk, as well as arrows painted on signs, poles and buildings guide the way. Logroño is a city of surprises, including a bingo parlor, beautiful ornate gates and art work. After the quiet of the countryside, it feels like a concrete jungle, especially to my feet. I see many of my Pilgrim friends, including the two ladies who helped me find my way in the dark leaving Viskarret.

A blue bridge takes me over the railroad tracks. A second bridge takes me over the highway and drops me into a peaceful park with swans floating in a small pond. The path has turned into patterned brick, which after the long concrete walk is extra hard on my feet. Crossing through a tunnel, the path returns to gravel—to the relief of my feet—and leads to a lake that supplies water to the city.

After skirting the lake, the route climbs to the vineyards. Because it's spring, the vines are short and stubby, budding tender green leaves. Green ribbons of growth contrast sharply with the red dirt. Nearing Navarette, I see a stand of trees planted in perfect lines. Their similar size indicates they were planted at the same time. They tower above me, trunks bare of branches, saving their green for the top, making them look like giant identical lollipops waiting to welcome me home for the evening.

I cross one more bridge, over one more highway, and pass ancient ruins. Their foundation footprints are all that remain of their former magnificence. A few steps down the path is a modern vineyard which must have a marketing genius on staff. With the precision of a surgeon, someone put a lot of time, thought and money into creating the photo opportunity for the vineyard. Talk about non-subliminal advertising. I celebrate genius in all forms, even when it is found in gross commercial advertising on the Camino.

Across the street, where a concrete pad has been poured, someone painted a yellow symbol of a camera to indicate the proper place for the photographer to best capture their photo. With your subject properly placed, and you standing in your assigned spot, you can now see the vineyards, their name elegantly written in white letters on a black ground. What an amazing way to advertise the vineyard. As my Irish friend would say, "Brilliant!"

Despite many photo stops and a snack in Logroño, my pace remains steady at the 3+/- km per hour. Navarette is a small town, and like most villages on the Camino, the route passes the local church and town square. Just past a barricade blocking the Camino, I can see the pension that I had failed to reach this morning. I haven't seen or heard from Sheelagh all day. My feet are back to killer mode, so I follow the path of least resistance and book myself a room at the Rey Sancho Hotel. It is the last building before the barricade. It took a blocked phone line and a construction zone to lead me to this hotel. Who am I to argue with the Universe?

It's 3:45 when I reach my room. Always, my first order of business is to connect with Gerald. Next on the agenda is to wash my shirt and socks and hang them in the open window, in hopes that they will be dry in the morning. It's a trick I learned from Dennis. After a quick shower, I'm ready to find some food and my friends. I know Dennis is staying somewhere in town and hope that Sheelagh has made it.

The square is next to the hotel, so I head there. The first person I see is Dennis enjoying a glass of wine at an outdoor café. Our reunion is interrupted by his daily 6:00 p.m. call to his wife. With the time difference, they are able to talk before she goes to work.

Stepping aside to give him some privacy, I move towards the fountain. In short order, I'm surrounded by Baly and Jose (Paris Pilgrims who also stayed in Orrison), Phillip and Anne, brother and sister from England, Sheelagh and a German girl whose name I don't know, but she was a part of a group photo taken with me this morning in Logroño. We wait on Dennis before deciding where to eat.

From this crowd, only Dennis, Phillip, Anne and I choose to eat together. The others scatter in different directions. The four of us enter an arched hallway heading under my hotel and discover a door to the hotel's restaurant located in the basement. It is tastefully decorated with modern fixtures that blend nicely with the medieval architecture. We are the only ones here, either because it's early, or the size of the town or masterful orchestration by Heaven above. Which of these is correct, I will never know, but the evening gets wacky in a hurry.

After an awkward amount of time, we're greeted by a tall, outgoing Spaniard who claims to be the cook, but looks and acts like a slightly bulkier version of John Cleese in *Monty Python*. The waiter has not shown up for work, so our cook is pulling double duty for the evening. His demeanor is outlandish. At one point he demands to switch places with Dennis, sits in Dennis' chair and pretends to order from Dennis, our new cook/waiter. The entire evening feels like an outtake from one of those TV shows with hidden cameras. Except the only person who comes out of hiding is a waiter, finally showing up for work late. The food is delicious, the company even better, and the four of us experience the meal of a lifetime. Bonus: For a 2 euro donation, I receive four pieces of ice to soak my feet in the bidet in my room.

Day 11

Stages 8 & 9 - Navarette to Azofra
22.2 km (13.8 miles)

This morning I'm up by 5:30 and out the door before 7:00. Walking in the cooler temperature, without direct sun, is my best time to lay tracks on the day. Everything feels fresh, and usually I'm walking alone. By mid-morning I know others will begin to pass me. People who start from my starting point but leave after me, or those who travel farther while walking really fast. But until then, the solitude of the trail with the shifting light of the awakening sun is the best part of the day.

The La Rioja region feels different from the region of Navarre. I didn't really feel it yesterday, probably because of the hustle and bustle of Logroño, but this morning the trail feels subtly different. Maybe it's the deep red of the earth, broken only by the stunted growth of spring grape vines. Or perhaps it's the blank blue slate of a cloudless sky, or the lack of civilization. I'm not sure and really don't care why it feels different today, except to acknowledge it and honor it.

The views are incredible, which is both good news and bad news. Good news, you can see the next town and spot a foot rest, food stop or bathroom break up ahead. Bad news, the views are so spectacular it can take a long time to get there. At my pace, sometimes hours.

As I get closer to Ventosa, the silence of the morning is

shattered by barking dogs. Although I can't see them yet, I picture a group similar to the shaggy hounds lounging outside of Los Arcos. The source of their unhappiness is unclear, but whatever it is, they are relentless in voicing their displeasure.

By 8:30, I'm planted in a bright red chair, pulled up to a bright red table outside of the Buen Camino, a café-bar in Ventosa. The only other patron is a tall, lanky, reserved Swedish man named Per. With a nod and "Buen Camino," we both retreat to our own thoughts. As I sit and enjoy my breakfast and roll my feet on my racquetball, a parade of Pilgrims begins coming down the trail.

Just as I'm preparing to head out, Baly and Jose arrive. Baly's shoulders are aching and she's not feeling well. Rather than leave as intended, I hand her the magic stick and wait until she's feeling better before continuing on my way. Leaving town, I pass another fenced vineyard. This one doesn't have a marketing genius on staff, but they do make an attempt to encourage consumption along the way. The small sign, with a picture of a leather Pilgrim flask says, "Pilgrim Enjoy Rioja Wine on the Way" and "*Peregrino Disfruta del Vino de Rioja en el Camino.*"

My intention is to spend the night in Nájera tonight, another 9-plus km away, which will put me into town with plenty of time to rest this afternoon. The guidebook shows the population of Nájera to be 8,500, which means there are choices of places to stay, but it is a stage end on my guidebook, so I expect it to be busier than the past few villages I've stayed in.

With the exception of a steep, rocky climb up a dry ravine, the path is wide and smooth. The soft gravel cushions my feet. Two weeks ago, I had no idea how much difference the road surface would make to my body. And, I surely would not have labeled it as soft. Like everything else, experience has changed my perception.

Storm clouds gather above distant hills. Hills that beckon, their dark blue outline separating the cloudy sky from the red dirt. The weather is near perfect, leaning toward the warm side. My white shirt has a built-in hood that I can pull over my hat to protect my neck from the sun. But pulled up, it blocks the wind and I heat up. It's a tradeoff of breeze versus sun protection. There is no shade, no trees to speak of in this farm and ranchland.

My guidebook has a picture of a delightful beehive building that is located in Nájera, and sure enough, here it is, looking exactly like the picture.

Until you go inside. Inside, the building is covered in graffiti. I take time to look out the stone window and imagine the multitude of people who have done the same, and I feel connected to their energy. After my two-minute tour, which is an exaggeration, I take a break on a wooden bench outside to rest for a few minutes.

When I leave, coming around the corner, I see Baly and Jose again. Each time we see each other is a joyous occasion, even when it has only been a few hours. Together we cross a wooden bridge over a small stream and enter the outer margin of the city. Crammed between inspiring Camino signs and graffiti are advertisements. Some are full blown billboard signs; others really are graffiti, like the advertisement for massages (*masajes*), spray painted on a concrete pillar. They are a source of irritation or relief, depending on my need of their service, but mostly, they are an eyesore. The graffiti has been one of the biggest shocks of the Camino.

Nájera feels busy compared to the quiet of the countryside. Cars and people crowd the trail. On a side road to my left, I see Anne and Phillip weaving in and out of stores. Catching up to them to say "Hi," I discover they are planning a picnic by the river and accept their invitation to join them. My sweet tooth is aching, so I stop and purchase dessert before meeting them at the park next to the river. They make room on their bench and the three of us enjoy the view.

To our left, the road crosses the river above our head. From our bench, we can see cars and Pilgrims as they cross. Glancing up, we see Sheelagh on the bridge. She stops, turns towards us to take a picture of the river, and the three of us go into a wild dance, waving our arms, shouting, trying to get her attention. She has no clue we are here. Our shouts can't compete with the noise of the river, passing cars and city sounds. We watch as Sheelagh takes several more pictures and then continues on her way

It's 1:00 by the time we finish lunch. Though I had planned to stay here tonight, I don't like the feel of this town. My feet are feeling pretty good, despite the single blister I found during lunch, so I decide to press on. Azofra, the next village, is less than 6 km away, and based on my past few days' performance, I think I can make it by early afternoon.

The guidebook shows the elevation as a gentle climb with one small peak between Nájera and Azofra. After the edge of town, the path returns to wide smooth gravel. The countryside looks like a patchwork quilt of red and green. As I climb a small rise, the silence is interrupted by the sound of bleating sheep, twinkling bells and dogs barking instructions to the flock. I can't see them; they are on the other side of the barn wall. But the animals bark and bleat in waves, one group setting off another group. I suspect it is a large flock, because it sounds like a sheep convention.

Either my pace has been terrific, or my time was off in leaving Nájera, because I have difficulty believing that I covered the 5.8 km in 75 minutes. But here it is, 2:15 in the afternoon and I'm crawling into Azofra. My feet hurt. My butt hurts. I'm hot and exhausted. The guidebook says the population of Azofra is 250, but from the looks of it, that count may be generous. Supposedly, I have three choices of places to sleep tonight. The next town is 10 km away and my legs and feet are spent, so this is it. I'm done. I'm cooked. I'm not going any further.

Rather than try the alburgues, I head straight to the Real Casona de las Amas, listed as an "exclusive hotel" from 80 euros per night. Dragging myself into the entry, I receive a less than enthusiastic greeting from the man at the front desk.

"Do you have a room for the night?" I ask.

"*Si.*"

"How much is it?"

"Ninety euros per night."

"Oh. Does it have a bathtub?"

"No."

"Oh well, never mind." As I turn to go, I stop and ask, "You mean to tell me you don't have a room with a bathtub in this place?"

"Oh, *si, señora,* but it cost 120 euros."

"Done."

My key is attached to another oversized tassel, red this time. The building feels like a former estate home. We ride the elevator to the second floor and step into a landing area. I see a gigantic painting of a mother and child riding on a cloud. Some kind of silver decorative incense bowl is sitting on a skin rug under the painting. I'm enchanted by the hand-carved wooden door that looks four feet wide and the wooden beams in the ceiling.

A walkway opens into the room, and I see two matching twin beds snuggled together in the center of the room with fancy wooden head and foot boards. On each side of the beds, round tables hold red-shaded lamps. The table on the left has a vintage black candlestick telephone.

The tapestry, centered above the two beds, matches the heavy drapes. The white linen bedcovers match the white sheers in the window. Worn but exquisite rugs dot the wood floors.

The bathroom has been painted a cheerful yellow. A small window lets in light above a modern corner garden tub. A copper sink mounted in a marble counter top is topped by a large hand-carved, wooden mirror. There is no bidet, which is fine by me. I have a garden tub!

As soon as I'm left alone, I strip, wash underwear and socks and hang them from the clothes line I've strung between the light fixtures on either side of the mirror. I fall asleep in the bathtub, again. I wake up and crawl into bed for the night by 5:15. No dinner. No exploring. No nothing. Just laundry, bath and bed. I do know one thing. Exclusive is a nicer word for expensive.

Day 12

Stages 9 & 10 - Azofra to Redecilla del Camino
26.3 km (16.34 miles)

I didn't get out of bed until 5:45 this morning. I can't tell if the cost of my "exclusive" room was a total waste or a great investment. However, after being horizontal for twelve hours, I feel like a new woman. My daily morning routine has two additional tasks this morning. The second flap cover removal and treatment of my gums goes smoothly, and then I add blister care for the blister that formed on the top of my left foot. The location seems odd and I have no idea where it came from.

I'm out the door by 7:15. My first photo of the day is my exclusive hotel in the early dawn light. The plain exterior hides the opulent interior and makes me wonder what treasures are hidden behind the ancient walls I've passed on this trip.

The only other person I see on the road at this hour is my breakfast companion from yesterday. Per and I walk together for a while, but my slower gait and frequent photo stops do not match his pace. A "Buen Camino" and he's gone, ever increasing the distance between us, until he is lost on the horizon.

The 10-km hike to the next town flows through lush green fields and striped vineyards, interspersed with fields of the bright yellow flowers I first saw coming into Pamplona. As it turns out, they are called Rapeseed, or Canola, and are grown to process into biodegradable oil for cars. Who knew that the Camino would be a source of education and inspiration for fossil fuel alternatives?

At the top of a steep hill, I see three young men selling trinkets, drinks and snacks for a "donation." The men are charming and have the easy confidence of polished salesmen. Famished from my lack of dinner last night, I drop two euros in their bucket in exchange for an orange juice. Next to their car is a Pilgrim camp, and I wobble over to sit on one of its concrete benches to rest briefly before setting off again.

The last hill into Cirueña is the steepest of the day, or at least it feels that way. To my left, I notice a strange looking building and realize it's a driving range. WHAT? A short walk farther, I see the greens and fairways of the Rioja Alta Golf Club. It's hopping with business on a Sunday morning.

As I pass by, I notice a "Welcome Pilgrim" breakfast sign, but dismiss the idea of stopping. But before I can take five steps, I receive a powerful message to stop, go back and eat. Trusting the instructions from my inner guidance system, I turn back. I smile at the idea that my Camino will include breakfast with a golf-course view. Simply amazing.

I'm not the only Pilgrim, but I am the only woman in the room. Removing my backpack and sticks, I sit down and pull out my guidebook to see if the golf course is on the map. Sure enough, there it is. Map reading has never been my strong suit. So far, I've been looking for fonts, red exclamation points, cafés and places to sleep. Now, I realize, perhaps I should take more time each day and try to figure out what all those other squiggly lines on the map mean.

After breakfast, I continue on my journey and am struck by the uniqueness of this town. All the houses look new but empty. The only people I've seen thus far were at the golf course, and the majority looked Asian instead of Spanish. Even though Sunday mornings are quiet in Spain, this is an eerie, deserted quiet. At the far side of the town's edge, I see a young couple playing in a small park with their toddler. I hope they are a sign that people really do occupy this town.

The storm clouds that threatened earlier have delivered on their promise. A light rain begins falling, making it necessary to adapt to new conditions. No wind blowing, so the poncho is all I need to stay dry. Legs really don't matter in a light rain, because the quick-dry pants really do dry quickly.

The route to Santo Domingo de Calzada is a gradual decline that provides views that seem to go on forever. Every time I think it can't get any more beautiful, I see something new that alights the child in me to clap her hands with glee. This afternoon, a single red poppy standing among luscious green grass reminds me to embrace my authenticity.

By 11:30, I've reached Santo Domingo de Calzada, or Santo Domingo for short. In four hours I've already walked 15-plus km today. My pace is picking up. When I thought Cirueña looked deserted this morning, I had no idea what deserted looked like. At least in Cirueña, there were people on the golf course and in the park. But here, in Santo Domingo, it's downright spooky. This town is larger, and absolutely devoid of life. Anywhere. Like, off the charts, *Planet-of-the-Apes* empty. No cars are moving. No dogs or cats can be seen or heard. I even step out in the middle of the street, tempting fate to stir up some action, but I don't see another living soul.

Getting closer to the center of town, an inviting café on my right looks like a good place to eat and get out of the rain. At last I see signs of life. The café is crowded from the weather. It's a gathering place for locals and Pilgrims. Today is not a day to sit outside. Inside the café, I see my friend Justine, the Pied Piper, with two new companions, Chris and his Aunt Kate. Although their meal has already begun, they invite me to share their table. When they are done, they are out the door.

Facing the window, I enjoy watching the Pilgrims pass,

looking for people I know. One of them is Sheelagh. Quickly, I stick my head out the door to catch her, and this time she hears me. She joins me for lunch. We swap stories of what has happened in our lives since we last saw each other.

It is 1:15 by the time we finish lunch, and we consider touring the museum and cathedral. But there is a fee to do so and, ironically enough, a long line of people waiting for the tour. We discuss the merits of staying in Santo Domingo, or continuing onward, and quickly agree to keep moving.

We reach the next village, Grañón, by 3:00 and stop for a snack and facilities break. While resting, Sheelagh sees a friend who is staying in the local alburgue who is in search of bug spray because his bunk is jumping with bedbugs. My German roommate from Estella, Tanja, sees me and leaps in my lap for a hug. The frequency of reconnections are increasing and becoming more special because we are no longer strangers. At any point, we know we may not see each other again.

Sheelagh and I have no intention of staying in a place that has bed bugs, so we say goodbye to our friends and hope the next town, Redecilla del Camino, offers better lodging. The temperature is dropping. The wind is picking up and it's still sprinkling. To keep my poncho from blowing, I tie my clothesline around the poncho and tie it in a bow under my belly pack. It may not be fashionable, but it's functional.

The path is a gradual incline, and I hope to find a place to stay soon. I'm feeling whipped. Entering town, what looks like a Vitex tree has grown up and over a wall and is loaded with purple blooms. They are a bright spot of color and welcome us to town.

As we pass through Redecilla, we see a casa rural sign on a building that looks like a bar. It promises better accommodations than an alburgue, but before committing, we ask to see the room. We are led up two flights of narrow stairs to a clean and homey room with rose-colored walls. There are two double beds, a private bath and plenty of space to put our stuff. I'm relieved that we have found our home for the night.

The barkeep has Irish connections, and she and Sheelagh really hit it off. This casa rural offers laundry services, so I hobble up the stairs, shower, change into my pajamas and then head back down to the bar to hand over my dirty clothes. They are promised to be done by 9:00 tonight.

Sheelagh and I enjoy a snack, access to WI-FI and front-row seats to Sunday night life in a Spanish village of 150 people. The table across from us is filled with four Spanish men playing a card game. Two more men watch a *fútbol* game with intensity. At times, noise erupts from one of the players and cards start slapping the table. At other times, the men sit quietly, with fierce looks of concentration on their faces. I have no idea what they are playing, but it's fascinating to watch.

Sheelagh and I are joined by a Pilgrim from Lithuania, who also knows our Italian friend, Andrea. We order another round of beer and notice that the card game has been replaced by a hen party. Three women of various ages now occupy the table, whispering conversations over cups of coffee. They are not loud like the men but are equally interesting.

Sheelagh heads to the room, but I stay in the bar to upload pictures to the cloud, roll my feet and wait on laundry. Tanja and Jessica come into the bar for a drink. They are staying in an alburgue down the street. Nine o'clock comes and goes, but no laundry. Sigh. The *new* promise is that they will be ready overnight and tied in a bag onto our door for an early morning start. There is nothing I can do, so I head up to the room. I'm not ecstatic about the situation, and recognize I MAY have some control issues. Rather than focus on the negative, I go to bed to dream of the joy I will feel when I wake up in the morning to my bag of clean laundry.

Email to Richard:

I walked 26.3 km to Redecilla del Camino in a light rain and at times, blowing wind. The country is absolutely beautiful. I'm learning how to listen to my body and take care of it along the way. Last night I stayed at an expensive hotel and stayed in bed for almost 12 hours. The room had a bath and I was hurting. It was an investment in myself.

I am so glad that Ryan continues to help you and hope the items he's sending will allow you to gain your freedom. It will come. It's only a matter of time. In the meantime, keep taking care of yourself and stay strong.

Love you

Day 13

Stages 10 & 11 - Redecilla del Camino to Villafranca Montes de Oca
23.7 km (14.73 miles)

My dream was but a dream. There is no bag of clothes hanging from the door. It's early, not most Spaniard's favorite time of the day, and when I tiptoe down into the bar, it's empty. I try several doors to find someone, but can't rouse anyone's attention. The challenge of missing clothes is a perfect opportunity for me to GRIPP Life, be grateful and accept reality.

After several trips up and down the stairs, OK, maybe a little stomp or two, a woman whom I haven't seen before appears. She has a worried look on her face, leads me by the hand to her private area of the building to show me a washer and dryer. My very damp clothes are in the dryer. From gestures and occasional words, I understand that despite many attempts, the clothes haven't dried and that she wants to make another pass at drying them. In exchange for the wait, she agrees to provide a free breakfast for Sheelagh and me.

As we're eating, Justine and her followers roll in and out. By 8:30, the clothes are dry. After handing me the bag of clothes, I take the hospitalera by the hand, look her in the eye and thank her for her help. Her face melts with relief. Feeling grateful didn't make my clothes dry faster, but it did allow me, and those around me, to enjoy the morning while I waited.

Each morning is a mini-strategy session for the upcoming

day. How far should I walk today? What is the topography? Where will I eat, work my feet and find indoor plumbing? Today, Belorado looks like a great lunch stop and is only 11 km away. In between, there are tiny villages situated in quick succession, with the longest stretch between the third village and Belorado. Knowing this, I plan to make my first bathroom break in the second or third village. Planning this way has kept me successful on my quest for indoor plumbing for the past thirteen days of walking. Counting the number of villages has been the key to my success. Because as I reach each village, I can assess my needs and take appropriate action.

The first village is only 1.7 km from Redecilla del Camino. Sheelagh and I take our time photographing the unique colors, shapes, landscape and building materials of the homes as we pass through the village. The variety of architecture is fascinating.

The second village is only 1.8 km from the first village, but by the time we arrive my tummy is rumbling in protest and has communicated its need to stop. Unfortunately, this small village doesn't have any cafés or bars. There is only one alburgue in town, and it's closed for cleaning to prepare for the next wave of Pilgrims that will arrive in a few short hours. Checking my map, I see the next village, Vilamayor del Rio, is 3.4 km away and has a restaurant. Determined to keep my promise to myself, I pick up the pace. By the time we enter Vilamayor, I'm almost blind with need. The restaurant is locked up tight. Standing on the porch, rattling the door in desperation, I hope to raise someone to open the door. Through the windows, I can see beautifully set tables waiting for their guests, but not a single person.

Desperate, my eyes wild in search of an alternative, I notice the building next door has a wide inviting stone porch and looks like it could be a bed and breakfast. The building is comprised of two rectangular buildings stuck together. The front rectangle is a stone two-story building with a second-story porch made of wood sitting above the columned front porch. Wooden beams around the many windows add old-world charm. The short side of the front rectangular building is attached to the long side of a three-story, yellow stucco building. The front door is wide open, beckoning me to break and enter.

Without hesitation, I dive into the building, yell "*Hola?*" to an empty room. Across from the front door is a sink, and to the right is an open door to a bathroom. Dropping my pack next to a red velvet chair, I rush through the bathroom door, removing my belly pack on the way to save time.

It's a close call. From inside the bathroom, I can hear Sheelagh greeting someone; the man's voice sounds friendly. What a relief. After I'm through, Sheelagh takes her turn in the bathroom, and I wait for her in the now empty lobby. Whoever Sheelagh spoke to has left. As I gaze around the room, I wonder what its purpose is. I can tell it's not a bed and breakfast. The walls are an attractive blue, spotted by various vintage photographs. To my right is an expansive bar area. A warm, hand-carved buffet leans against a brick wall, and dozens of wine bottles line one entire wall. In front of the buffet is a marble-topped counter with stunning tile trim on its façade. A closed door leads to who knows where? What is this place?

Sheelagh re-joins me and thinks there is someone coming to talk to us, and that it was OK to use the facilities. Thank goodness. Moments later, a darling man comes through the closed door on my left. He's wearing a white coat topped by a red bandana tied casually around his throat. His brown hair is nicely styled and matches his sparkling brown eyes. His engaging smile reveals braces. He seems genuinely glad to see us and speaks perfect English.

We have stumbled into a ham factory, which explains the pig on the sign on the front porch. I thought it was folk art, but it turns out that it is the name of the company. This young and handsome man is the owner's son and just happens to be here today because he's visiting his family and has an appointment with his local dentist. He lives in London, which explains his perfect English, and his haircut.

Spain is renowned for its fine ham, and this factory still uses ancient techniques to cure its ham. His pride in what they do is evident. He invites us to tour the factory. Sheelagh and I look at each other and both nod our heads. We follow the man through a doorway that leads to the three-story side of the building. Through a glass window, we see thousands of ham legs tied to green ropes, hanging from the ceiling.

We walk down two short flights of stairs and enter the actual factory. The floor is painted bright green, and we're surrounded by suspended hams. OK, let's be real here, pig legs—some with black toenails, others with white toenails. From what I can tell, ancient technique means hanging legs from the ceiling in controlled temperatures for a long, long time. Oh, to be clear, it smells better than a Rudy's Bar-B-Q at home, and I'm pretty sure I will smell like ham for the rest of the day. The tour is surreal. Growing up in the suburbs, I never dreamed I would be in Spain, walking under hanging pig legs, with a vegetarian, who by the way seems fine.

After the tour, we return to the front room which, as it turns out, is a tasting room. Earlier, in soaking up the essence of the room, I failed to notice two pig legs, side by side, toes pointed to the sky, shackled inside their custom metal frames, sitting on the marble counter top. The racks remind me of foot rests in a gynecological office.

When we're offered a taste of ham, Sheelagh turns white. I know her well enough by now to know that she is struggling with the decision to decline the taste, or suffer through a bite. Our tour guide generously cuts three pieces. There is joy on his face and he is excited about sharing this gift with us. And although I love the taste of ham, I must confess, I have never eaten it in front of its own feet before. Sheelagh swallows hard, and rather than have her suffer, I volunteer to eat her slice and inform our gracious host that she is a vegetarian. It's the second time today I've seen a look of relief cross someone's face. The ham is delicious with a rich, buttery taste.

While I'm eating, our host asks, "How did you get in?" When we tell him the door was open, confusion crosses his face. The value of the inventory and the need to control the curing process makes it absolutely crucial to have secure doors that preclude visitors, like us, from just walking in willy-nilly.

"The door is never unlocked or open," he informs us.

We thank our host for his generosity, make one more trip to the bathroom and then gear up for the road. Before we can leave, our host must press a button to unlock the door to let us out.

This bathroom break has taken more than an hour. My

stubborn insistence to use indoor plumbing provided a ticket to this unique experience. The next 4.9 km fly by. Between bouts of laughter, Sheelagh and I take turns recounting our perspective of the ham tour.

The Camino route typically passes by the village church, and Belorado is no different. What is different about the Belorado church is the limestone cliff with ancient cave dwellings rising above it. The cave dwellings have received a modern conversion and are so unusual it is worth the extra steps to circle around the church and get a closer look at the caves.

On the other side of the church, a brick wall leads to a driveway which is blocked by an iron-bar gate. Hoping to get a closer look at the caves, we make our way up the road to peer through the gate's bars. A huge dog greets us. He has the coloring of a German Shepherd and the body of a Mastiff, looks to weigh at least 80 pounds and has the presence of a puppy. As we near the gate, the dog sticks his nose though the bars, sits down and wags his tail. His massive size is alarming, but his body language pleads, "Please, pet me!" Trusting my instincts, I reach out to pet him though the fence.

Sheelagh and I are simpatico in taking our time to enjoy the beauty of the lush landscape lining the driveway and the mystery of the caves above us. Reluctantly, we leave our captivating canine friend and the serenity of the moment to continue on our path. It is now after noon, and we are hungry.

We return to the church and find the yellow arrow to direct us to the next stage of our journey. Following the arrows through the village, we're drawn to a narrow side street that leads to a wide square. There, we locate a promising restaurant. While enjoying pizza and beer, we discuss our plan for the afternoon. Belorado is the destination for Stage 10 in the Brierley book, and not the place we want to spend the night. Turning the page, we see that Stage 11 ends in St. Juan de Ortega, which is 24.2 km away, too far for an afternoon walk. Between Belorado and St. Juan are four villages and a steep, steep climb. All of the villages are before the climb, so Sheelagh and I agree to walk as far as we can, to get as close to the mountain as possible. We'll make the steep climb in the morning when we are fresh.

By 1:30, we set out on the road again. Leaving Belorado behind us, we are welcomed by lush green landscape and cloudy skies. Darkening clouds promise rain. We blow through the first village and stop to rest in Villambistia. As we enter the small hamlet, on the right is a rectangular stone church with a bell tower. The blue painted wooden door offers an invitation to enter but is locked. My Soul is charmed by this place, and I ask Sheelagh to take my picture to capture the memory and the feeling of peace.

The skies open up with their promised rain as we prepare to leave Villambistia. Sheelagh needs to make a pit stop. Rather than wait, I set off to the next village, confident that she can easily catch me. When I arrive in Espinosa del Camino, I'm surprised to arrive alone. While waiting for Sheelagh, I check out the two alburgues in town, but I'm not comfortable with either accommodation. Chilled from the rain, I huddle under my poncho in front of an alburgue, and wait. Several Pilgrims pass by. Their unasked questions are plainly visible, but following Camino protocol, they offer a "Buen Camino" and keep walking.

When Sheelagh arrives, she explains she was sidetracked at the alburgue by a conversation with Justine. We consult the map and make the decision to continue together to Villafranca Montes de Oca, another 3.4 km. Sheelagh agrees with my assessment of our current options. We're counting on the map's accuracy for better accommodations in the next village.

So much has changed in such a short amount of time. Less than two weeks ago, I was beat just walking 8 km up the hill to Orrison. Today, I've already walked 20 km. It is raining and we have a hill to make it up and over before we reach our destination tonight. And, I am confident I can make it.

As we climb over the rise, the rain stops. Blue skies are filled with white fluffy clouds, and the beauty of the landscape is breathtaking. We can see the next village from the top of the rise. It appears closer than it really is, which makes the end of the day feel even longer.

When we finally arrive in Villafranca Montes de Oca, we book a double room at the first casa rural we pass and spend the evening resting. We're exhausted from the long day, and the rain has returned in buckets. One of Sheelagh's ankles has started to ache and she is unsure if she'll be able to walk tomorrow. Despite our growing abilities, tomorrow's hill on the map is intimidating and we have no idea what to expect.

Sheelagh accepts my offer of compression socks and wrestles her way into them. I take a Tylenol with Codeine, which was prescribed for my teeth but works wonderfully for road fatigue.

Our room is located at the front of the casa rural and sits next to the N-120. For the first time since my departure, I hear the sound of screeching brakes as trucks slow down to make a hard turn directly under my window. Tomorrow is a big day, and I will be faced with a decision. Do I move forward on my own or stay with a wounded friend?

Path leading into Villafranca Montes de Oca

Day 14

Stages 11 & 12 - Villafranca Montes de Oca to Atapuerca
18.5 km (11.5 miles)

The Tylenol helped with the pain last night, but I didn't wake up until after 7:30. I'm feeling groggy and grumpy about the slow start, or maybe it's residual from the Tylenol. My feet really hurt this morning. But after rolling them on the ball they feel almost brand new. My shoes feel tight, so I've loosened the toe box of my shoes to ease the discomfort. Recognizing that I'm off-kilter in my vibration doesn't make it go away.

Sheelagh has rallied so we will continue to walk together today. We've agreed to stop for breakfast at the San Anton Abad Hotel. We considered booking a room there last night but were too exhausted to walk the extra steps to get there. My plan is to enjoy a hot breakfast and a change of attitude, so that I can make the climb over the mountain with Ease and Grace.

Unfortunately, my plan fails *miserably*. Since we didn't have WI-FI last night, we both jump on the Internet to connect with our loved ones at home. I become irritated on this reliance on technology instead of enjoying each other's company during meals together. The hotel staff is unfriendly and service is slower than normal. We have to ask for our food twice and when it arrives, it isn't what I wanted. Rather than try a third time, I wash the dry toast down with a cup of hot chocolate. A quick trip to the bathroom and we're off, me with a worse attitude than before.

At the edge of town, the path turns into a rocky trail between a brick wall on the left and trees on the right. As the trail climbs, we can see a stucco house rising above the wall. We can hear the sound of a man singing, but can't see him until we climb past the house and turn around. In doing so, we enjoy a breathtaking view of the church spire. My Spirit begins to lift.

For the most part, Sheelagh and I have the path to ourselves. Occasional Pilgrims pass us, and we pass others who have stopped for a rest. The Camino is a magical place of fraternity. People coming together with a common goal to reach Santiago and, for the most part, are on a Spiritual quest. But that doesn't mean you want to spend time with everyone you meet.

Rather than hurt anyone's feelings, when faced with an unwelcome walking partner, I use my turtle pace, rest stops for my feet or stopping to take pictures to retain my solitude. Sheelagh has used power walking, which is how she believes she injured her ankle. As we climb the hill, we're joined by a man who wants to join us, but whose presence is unwelcome. Since power walking is out, we stop so often to take pictures that he grows frustrated and forges on without us.

As Sheelagh and I climb the hill, I realize that both of us have adopted a bad attitude today. Sheelagh's ankle is hurting and I haven't recovered from my morning grumpy. The path is steep and I'm back to twelve steps followed by three breaths. Determined to change the energy, I suggest we take a "gratitude" walk. Huffing and puffing up the hill we begin to exchange our gratitude.

"I am grateful for the beautiful weather."

"I am grateful for the shade of the trees."

"I am grateful for your company."

"I am grateful that I can walk."

"I am grateful for the smoothness of this trail."

We don't stop until a pair of Spanish men joins us at the top of the hill.

One Spaniard, Felix, is enthralled by my tall, blonde, Irish friend and immune to our not-so-subtle hints. He has slowed his pace to join us and sent his friend ahead by himself. Felix is a charming man. He's wearing a bright red shirt under a small day pack and carrying a wooden walking stick. His bald head and engaging smile remind me of a leprechaun. We discover he's an architect walking one day of the Camino to reach Atapuerca. He and his friend will return home tomorrow afternoon after visiting the prehistoric caves that were declared a UNESCO World Heritage site in 2000.

As we walk, his phone rings often and he conducts long conversations in Spanish. Sheelagh's rudimentary Spanish and heart of gold is enough to communicate with him in a multi-language conversation. I have no idea how much they understand each other, but effort is being made on both sides. I'm content to lag behind, enjoying the scenery and my solitude.

Sheelagh's ankle is aching, so we stop to rest. Our gallant Spaniard pulls out some unknown cream, and despite Sheelagh's protest, he insists on rubbing it on her ankle. After her treatment, as we walk, he shares his snacks with us and regales us with stories of banditos who supposedly still live in the surrounding forest. When he discovers we have no reservations for the night, Felix whips out his phone and books us a private room in Atapuerca, in the alburgue where he has a reservation.

While waiting for Sheelagh to relieve her bladder, I do my best to bridge the language barrier with Felix. He asks about the angel pin on the front of my hat. The pin belonged to my father and I've been wearing it to honor my parents. After experiencing many miracles while working together, Dad embraced my belief of angels. He ordered a bunch of them to give away to special people, and the one on my hat was one of the last from his collection. As I describe the significance of the pin in my broken Spanish, a flood of unexpected grief engulfs my body. I turn to hide my tears.

When Sheelagh returns from her trip behind the bush, we continue our journey, the two of them in the lead with me bringing up the rear. Slowing down even more, I enjoy a good cry, blessing and releasing the grief. After it passes, I return to the morning's gratitude walk, this time specifically concentrating on those things I am grateful for that came from my parents.

We reach St. Juan de Ortega a little after noon. It's the end destination for Stage 11 in the Brierley book and shows the population of the hamlet to be 20. From all appearances, the book is accurate. There are a few falling down houses, one alburgue, one casa rural and one church undergoing reconstruction. A gathering area in front of the church has a handful of bright red tables and chairs sitting in full sun, filled with Pilgrims we know and others we don't. It feels like home as we reunite with Justine and her crew, Phillip and Anne from England and Dennis. We delight in our pictures to capture the memory of being together, aware that we may never see each other again.

Sheelagh sees her friend Oliver, a retired medic whose passion is helping Pilgrims keep their feet healthy on the Camino, and has him look at her ankle. I catch up with Dennis, Phillip and

Anne. Dennis and I tour the church, and I light a candle for my parents.

While Sheelagh and I are catching up with our friends, Felix has picked out a table along the edge of the square. He points for us to join him and looks unhappy when we decline. We invite him to meet our friends but he doesn't budge from the table. His attitude is alarming. His charm has disappeared. Sheelagh and I come to an unspoken agreement to outwait our new friend. In time, he waves goodbye. I have no doubt he'll be waiting for us at the alburgue, eager to manipulate our time.

Dennis is spending the night in the alburgue in St. Juan, so he's already home for the day. Sheelagh and I have another 6 km to go before we reach Atapuerca. The good news is that it is downhill. Before leaving, I make plans with Dennis to see him tomorrow night in Burgos. I get the name of his hotel and hope they have a room for me when I show up tomorrow without a reservation. From what I can tell, his lodging choices have been excellent, and I'm ready for a good night's sleep. Burgos is one of the largest cities on the Camino, 180,000 people, and copying Dennis' Camino playbook is much less daunting than finding a place on my own in such a large city.

Oliver, the foot specialist, joins us on our walk, along with two college men from London. The conversation is fun and refreshing. The weather is perfect for walking, and in record time, we reach the next village of Ages, a darling village with a welcoming feel. In addition to the usual medieval charm, modern art pieces are sprinkled throughout town. Red flowers sitting on windowsills bring bright spots of color to the rock walls. The men are staying in Ages. Sheelagh and I are tempted to stay, especially after Felix's behavior at lunch, but we do have reservations in a private room, and our destination is only 2.5 km away.

While Sheelagh is getting last-minute instructions on her ankle from Oliver, I sit down on the edge of a rock wall to rest. As soon as I sit, my butt catches on fire; it feels like a stinging nettle. I jump up looking for a scorpion or other stinging bug, but don't see anything suspicious.

With the exception of my butt on fire, the walk into Atapuerca is uneventful. Coming into town, we take goofy pictures together before heading to the alburgue. It is 4:30 by the time we arrive, and the first person I see is Justine, sitting on a chair, soaking up the sun. Sheelagh waves to several people as we make our way through a maze of clothes lines, socks, underwear, pants and shirts flapping in the afternoon breeze. We are relieved to not see Felix, or his friend.

The hospitalera shows us our room, and we gratefully unpack our gear. Sheelagh heads out to see her friends, and I take advantage of the solitude to shower, roll my feet and rest. Today was relatively short, only 18.5 km, and with the exception of my still stinging butt, I feel pretty good.

Atapuerca is a tourist town of sorts and seems larger than the guidebook's claim of 200 people. Justine has invited us to dinner at another alburgue, but Sheelagh has committed to having dinner with her friend Frank and his two of his companions. I'm torn between choices. I would like to spend more time with Justine, but since I'm staying with Sheelagh, I decide to stick with her for dinner.

Frank is a jovial loud German. Daniel is a quiet Austrian with deep brown eyes that seem to absorb the room. I never catch the other German man's name; he sits at the other end of the table. Our International table companions are lively and fun. Dinner is delicious and filled with laughter.

After dinner, we return to the alburgue. Felix has been a non-issue, which is a relief. I catch up on correspondence with family and friends, first sending Richard an email and then checking messages. I'm greeted with a lovely surprise. My good friends from home, Thom and Jodi, husband and wife, have accepted my invitation to join me on the Camino. Both had indicated an interest in joining me for part of my journey but were limited by Jodi's school schedule. Jodi is a full-time student completing her Masters in Social Work degree. The message says they will arrive in Madrid on May 14th, spend a day in León and catch up to me. They are unsure if Thom will walk or not, but either way, we will be celebrating Thom's birthday on May 18th together.

Despite the rocky start to the day, the unexpected grief and my butt that is still on fire, today is the Best Day Ever! It has been a day of gratitude.

Standing Stones at Atapuerca

Day 15

Stage 12 - Atapuerca to Burgos
20.3 km (12.6 miles)

As usual, I'm ready before the sun comes up and Sheelagh is enjoying her bed. I suspect she enjoys the solitude of the room after I'm gone as much as I enjoy the solitude of the trail. We part ways with a big hug, and I set out on my own to enjoy the freshness of another day.

According to the map, once I cross the big hill after Atapuerca, it's downhill from there. The weather is perfect for walking today, cool with cloudy skies. Not the rain-threatening kind, friendly clouds that make you think you don't need sunscreen. At the edge of town, the trail turns right, straight up a red-dirt path that's scattered with rocks and boulders. It's one of the most difficult trails I've encountered on the Camino, which makes it all the more fun. I guess I'm weird in that the harder the trail the more enjoyable. At least for short stretches. I love the added element of adventure. It is a continuous climb between fenced green pastures filled with sheep. At the steepest point, the path becomes even rockier, and I slow down even more. It is an easy place to turn an ankle, and a difficult place to get help.

The majority of the morning is spent in solitude. I'm the only lone walker on the trail today; everyone else has been couples or small groups of Pilgrims. The peaceful ringing of sheep bells, the sheep's humorous *baas* and the rhythmic sound of my breathing put me in a zone of tranquility. A tranquility that is quickly shattered by the sound of loud voices, raucous laughter and *click-clack* of walking sticks. This is the first time the sound of my fellow Pilgrims has disturbed my enjoyment of the trail. Overcoming my desire to shout, "Shhhh!" I acknowledge my feelings and turn inward to discover why I'm giving my peace away.

At the top of the hill, even though I'm more than 15 km away, the view of Burgos is spectacular. There are several Pilgrims milling around, discussing which way to proceed. The guidebook shows several options, and the signs at the top of the hill are less than clear. After several minutes of discussion, one couple makes the decision to head left. Without a better plan, I follow them down the hill. Our paces are quite different, so I find myself quickly enjoying my solitude once again.

The downhill side of the mountain is very different from the uphill side. The fenced pastures of sheep and blue skies have been replaced by open fields of green grass and long-distance views of Burgos. The downhill path is less steep and less rocky. The careful uphill climb has changed to an easy, downhill march. It feels like a string is pulling me straight to Burgos.

Ironically, the sound of voices on this side of the mountain is welcome; it means I'm not lost. The uphill side was easy to navigate, but this downhill side is proving tricky. When I see a trio of Pilgrims—a girl with two guys—resting at a "Y" in the road, I'm happy to have some company. They are waiting for a friend who was having some foot problems.

After chatting awhile, my feet are ready to continue. As I prepare to leave, I'm surprised when the girl, Hannah, asks to join me, leaving her two male companions behind. She looks younger than my daughters and has a sweet energy. Hannah is from Canada and has an easy smile. Her presence is very welcome. We talk the entire way to Orbaneja, where we stop for a delicious breakfast. We come from different countries and different decades, but our childhood experiences are eerily similar. I'm in awe of our connection and how we came to walk together today.

After breakfast, without hesitation, Hannah heads for Burgos, and I'm right behind her. We talk when we can walk side by side and enjoy the silence when the trail narrows down to a single-file path. When I see the airport on our left, I realize we missed the turn for the river route. Rather than backtrack, we resign ourselves to a 6 km concrete hike.

As we pass Villafría, I know this is where Dennis will catch his bus to Burgos. He warned me about this section of the Camino and encouraged me to follow his example. For days, I've pondered his suggestion of taking the bus, arguing with myself back and forth. A part of me knows that character is built during tough times, and perhaps this section of the Camino has a lesson for me. Another part says, a 790-km walk is lesson enough, take the bus. Layered on top of this internal argument is the knowledge that I will be judged for taking the bus. And, I know the judgment has nothing to do with me, and everything to do with the person judging me, which makes the idea more appealing, because it offers a wonderful opportunity for growth for everyone. It takes courage to face negative judgments with love and compassion.

Walking into Burgos is actually fun for me. Between Hannah's company and my entrepreneurial background, I enjoy seeing the variety of businesses, especially the Las Vegas Hotel. That one made me smile. Hannah doesn't have plans for lodging tonight, but I'm on the hunt for the Hotel Centro. Nearing the edge of Burgos, my new friend and I part company. I stop to ask for directions. My Spanish is insufficient to understand the elaborate answers to my question. After failing to understand several people, I hire a taxi to take me to my destination. When I arrive five minutes later, at a cost of less than seven euros, I giggle.

The Hotel Centro is a modern-looking building on the outside and richly furnished on the inside. Patrons are nicely dressed, and

I'm conscious of my Camino gear and stench. I know girls aren't supposed to sweat, but we do. The Camino detoxifies the body and I stink, all the time, and most fiercely fresh from the road. Like now, standing in a beautiful hotel entryway, surrounded by beautiful nice-smelling, non-Pilgrim people.

It is only a little after noon and I'm already receiving a key to my room. Yippee! Dennis has not arrived yet, so I leave a message for him at the front desk with my room number. The room is divine, the bath even more heavenly. Despite a two-hour soak in the tub, I still stink, but at least I'm clean. My Compeed-brand blister cover has soaked off, but I can put on another one tomorrow. Since I've never used a bidet for its original intention, the idea of washing my clothes in it doesn't gross me out. I know the bidet has been cleaned between guests, and it's awfully handy to wash clothes in. With clean body, clean clothes hanging to dry, I lie down and enjoy a nap until Dennis calls me.

As it turns out, he's in the room around the corner from me; they must put all the Pilgrims on the top floor together. We enjoy a snack and a beer in the bar and soak up the ambiance of the Burgos social scene. Dennis knows how to pick a good hotel and shares his black book of reservations. The easiest way to copy them is to photograph them, and even though I feel like a stalker, I'm happy to have this rolodex of places to stay. After our beer, we set out for the cathedral. In every village on the Camino, the cathedral is the customary Pilgrim meeting place. I'm pleased, but not surprised, to see my Canadian friend Hannah sitting on a bench.

Dennis and I pay to take a tour of the cathedral. Outside the ticket office, beggars plead for money. They are the first I've seen on the Camino, and I'm fascinated that they choose to locate themselves here. Even though I've read Ken Follett's *Pillars of the Earth* and *World Without End*, and thought I knew what to expect, I'm unprepared for the majesty and artistry of this building. Murals on the ceilings. Paintings on the walls. Carved angels. Painted angels. Stained-glass windows. Bells ringing. Gold. Silver. A marble-carved sarcophagus with a poodle carved at the feet of its master. Golden robes. Golden staircases. Gold challises. Carved stone ceilings and walls. Marble floors. El Cid. Room after room, building after building, I'm overwhelmed by the size and opulence of this cathedral. It is too much for me to absorb at one time. The exit drops us back into the ticket office. I'm pleased, but not surprised, to see Sheelagh and Frank, from last night. They are about to take the tour. I relish these not-so-chance encounters and treasure each one.

After making plans to meet for dinner, Dennis heads back to the hotel to rest. I wander through a few of the shops to purchase food supplies for tomorrow's 21-km walk. There are only two stops between Burgos and Hornillos de Camino, so provisioning food today seems like a good idea. The "Meseta" or flats start tomorrow and will continue for the next ten days. I have heard they are boring, which is hard for me to imagine. The natural beauty of this country has seeped into my soul.

In my room, I catch up on my notes, send Richard an email and enjoy an unknown dessert from the bakery. Walking with Hannah today made me realize a difficult journey is much easier when you are connected heart to heart with a friend.

Around 6:30 p.m., Dennis and I set out to find a Pilgrim dinner. I'm shocked by the number of people walking the streets. When we toured the cathedral earlier, the streets were busy but not crowded. Now, it's difficult to navigate through the throng of young and old, walkers and strollers, pets on leashes and occasional cars. We make our way back to the square to find a restaurant. Dennis points out several but none suit my fancy. Wanting something different from the Pilgrim meal, I suggest a pizza/pasta restaurant I see across the square. Dennis agrees. As we enter the restaurant, I'm pleased to see Sheelagh and Frank having dinner. They make room for us and we share a deliciously different meal.

After dinner, Dennis and I say goodbye to Sheelagh and Frank and weave our way back to the hotel through the still busy streets by the light of the fading day. My feet are hurting from the extra walking this afternoon, and it's all I can do to make it back to the hotel.

I treat my gums and feet before calling it a day. My final thought is gratitude for the cuckoo birds that have greeted me for the past few days. I didn't know before the Camino that they were real birds, and not just clocks. *Cuckoo. Cuckoo.*

Email to Richard:

I made it to Burgos with Ease and Grace. Met a new girl on the trip and we talked the whole way into town. 10 km of industrial district. Car lots, Bridgestone tire company, Las Vegas Hotel! Burgos has a cathedral that was started in the 1300s and had continued construction for centuries. I've never seen anything like it.

Tomorrow I'm off to the "flat lands" for a few days. It will be time to listen to my music.

Hard to believe I've already completed 1/3 of the walk.

Love you.

Day 16

Stage 13 - Burgos to Hornillos del Camino
21 km (13 miles)

It was hot last night. After hours of tossing and turning, I finally got up and turned the air conditioner on. Yesterday's concrete walking took a toll, so every time I woke up, which was often, I stretched my legs up in the air, swung them from side to side, open, closed, pointed toes, stretched calves. I'm sure I looked ridiculous, but the stretching really helped ease the muscle fatigue. The beauty of a single room is that I can take care of myself without disturbing anyone else and not have to worry about how silly I look in doing so.

It's 5:30 a.m., and I'm wide awake, not pretending that I can go back to sleep. After an hour of stretching, packing and preparing for the day, I'm out the door by 6:45, in the pre-dawn light. Last night's hustle and bustle has been replaced with stillness. In a city of this size, I'm alone on the city streets and am humbled by the uniqueness of the moment. It is a gift to experience this moment of calm in the center of this urban mass. Taking a breath, I stop, dig my phone out of my pants and take a picture of the empty streets by lamplight.

As soon as I'm back on the Camino, I'm joined by fellow Pilgrims taking advantage of the morning coolness. The path passes by the cathedral, which is even more beautiful in the soft morning light. Burgos is filled with architectural masterpieces, and I stop to explore each one.

At the city's edge, an impressive ancient stone and brick wall continues to provide a barrier of protection around the city. The wall was built to last. There's no sign of aging on its dense thickness. The arched entryway has been utilized by modern road builders to allow automobile access through the wall, squeezing down to a single lane to do so. With the exception of the occasional Pilgrim, the streets are still quiet.

As I near the archway, I join two men who look lost. From our left, a cab suddenly pulls around the corner and a woman with a backpack climbs out. After paying the cabdriver, she joins our small group and shares that she had become lost in the maze of the city and hired the cab to put her back on the Camino. At least for now, we are in the right place.

Although my mapping skills are not the best, I intuitively know where to go, leading my fellow companions under the archway, through the outer neighborhoods and across the Rio Arlanzón. By the time we arrive at the N-120, the day has brightened, and there is little traffic on the road. At the corner, one arrow points towards the park and another towards the sidewalk running alongside the N-120. Without hesitation I enter the park. My companions continue to follow me. The park is quite large and it takes several minutes of walking on the wide, smooth, tree-lined path to reach the iron gate at the end. I recognize we're walking on the path that was filmed in *The Way*. It's the scene in which the gypsy boy is carrying Martin Sheen's backpack as punishment for stealing it. On a deeper level, my soles are following the footsteps of millions of souls who have come before me. I can feel their presence, supporting me on my quest.

At the end of the park, we turn right and reconnect to the sidewalk next to the N-120. Both arrows brought us to the same place, but the path I chose has been peaceful compared to the roadway walk. We cross the N-120 again, putting the city of Burgos behind us. The path is now unmistakable and my companions quickly outpace me, no longer needing my leadership, until they come to a "Y" in the road not marked.

Construction on the freeway at the convergence of a railroad line and freeway has caused their confusion. My map doesn't offer any guidance through the construction, so we follow my gut. Two turns later, we're back on a way-marked route. Once again, my companions' long, fast strides create a gap between us with each step they take. I'm reminded of the tortoise and the hare, and I am really enjoying being the tortoise.

The blue skies and white clouds offer a stark contrast to the green and red dirt of the earth. The sounds of the birds, dove and cuckoo, keep me entertained. My company is enough. At some point, I expect to experience an epiphany, but so far the rhythm of breathing and movement is a walking meditation, quieting the mind instead of revealing earth-shattering revelations.

In Tarjados, I stop for my second breakfast of the day. The rolls I purchased yesterday provided a handy snack before dawn this morning. With such few services on today's route, I buy a sandwich to go in addition to my breakfast. It's after 9:00 in the morning. I've logged 11 km on the day and have another 10 km to go before I reach Hornillos del Camino. At this pace, I'll have time to find a room, do laundry, take a nap and hopefully soak in a private bathtub.

My feet and legs are still aching from the concrete walking, and even though I'm slow compared to other Pilgrims, I'm breaking land-speed records for myself. Hitting the road early and stopping at a decent time are much more enjoyable than walking until 4:00 or 5:00 in the afternoon.

Dennis is staying in a hotel off the Camino. The hotel is sending a car to pick him up today and return him to Hornillos del Camino tomorrow morning. Knowing Dennis, the hotel will be lovely, but I don't like the idea of not being able to step right out my door and start walking, so I'm hoping to find a nice place in town. Hornillos is small—a population of 80 people, according to the guidebook. By arriving early, I hope to be able to find a place to stay. The next town is almost 6 km away and only has one alburgue.

Rabé de las Calzados, the only village before Hornillos, is only 2.3 km from Tarjados. The town has a beautiful fountain with four fonts, providing refreshing water for Pilgrims with a stylish flare. The narrow streets are like a maze. High walls and curved streets shorten my line of sight to the next curve.

Coming around a corner, I'm surprised to see Adam outside an alburgue, putting a bicycle together. I shouldn't ever be surprised on the Camino, but I've been following Adam on Facebook ever since we met on Day 4 in Larrasoañna. The last time I saw him was in Estella. According to his posts, Adam has been days ahead of me since then. Although I knew he was waiting on a bicycle to be delivered, I never thought I would catch up to him. And here he is, in the tiniest of villages, at the perfect time, to hug, Buen Camino and continue on.

Now that I'm officially on the Meseta, I can see the difference. The path is as straight and flat as I've seen it. Feels like I can see forever. Everything is green and lush, nothing like the pictures with dry brown grass. This drought-tolerant Texan is thrilled to see this sea of green. I cannot imagine anyone thinking this flat country as boring. Of course, I'm walking in the spring. I suspect this green will be dry, brown and dead by summer. I am grateful I have the ability to walk now.

Adam rides by, weaving like a drunken sailor on wheels. His backpack isn't designed for the bike, and he's still getting his legs under him. He hollers a "Buen Camino!" and saves himself from falling with a quick jerk of the wheel as he makes his way up the gentle rise.

The map shows a bit of hill to climb before reaching

Hornillos del Camino. The only place to stop and rest is in Fuente de Praotorre. The leaves from the small grove of trees seem to call my name and urge me to take care of myself. The only services provided are picnic tables, which is all I need to enjoy my sandwich, change socks and work the knots out of my feet. Sitting on top of the picnic table, using the bench to roll the ball on my feet, I see Dennis go by in a blur. I mentally give him a thumbs-up. Trying to gain his attention in the wind would have been a waste of time, and he looked like he was in his walking zone.

Leaving the picnic tables, I rejoin the route. The first person I see is Frank. Sheelagh is nowhere to be seen. Her ankle issues have returned, and she's fallen behind him on the trail.

The Camino is busier now, and we're in a steady flow of Pilgrims. Frank makes it clear that he intends to walk with me, but I prefer to walk alone. Using the stalling techniques of re-tying my shoes and taking pictures don't work. Frank stays with me until he sees a Pilgrim with a ukulele. Frank is offered the ukulele to play and begins to sing and strum the instrument. I'm happy that he has found someone to enjoy on the trail so I can drop back to enjoy my solitary journey.

As I near my final destination, I see the French couple that Sheelagh and I shared a room with on Day 4. Our reunions are always joyous, despite our inability to communicate with words. By the time we stumble into Hornillos del Camino at 12:45, I'm exhausted. Dennis is sitting in a chair, waiting for his ride, and we spend a few minutes chatting. I need to get horizontal, so I set off in search of a bed for the night. The casa rural on my left has a private room with two beds or a room with a single bed. My gut tells me to get the room with two beds, suspecting Sheelagh will show up and need a place to stay. If not, I will have paid a few euros extra for a larger room. Knowing that Sheelagh checks the Internet often, I send her a WhatsApp message, letting her know she has a bed for the night, if she needs one.

After a shower, which I'm grateful for, I give my clothes to the hospitalera to wash. As soon as they're ready, I hang them on the line in the backyard. The owners are adding onto their house, and as my clothes flap in the breeze, I watch the construction crane lift materials up and over a rock wall. Construction is a sign of prosperity, and I'm pleased to witness this family's growing business.

Sheelagh received my message and arrives happy to have a place to stay. We sit in the community den with Justine, Kate and Kris. The three of them have been traveling together as a trio for quite some time. In addition, we meet a new Pilgrim, Mandy, who is very knowledgeable in reflexology and is quite concerned about Sheelagh's Achilles tendon.

Instead of a Pilgrim meal, this casa rural provides the use of the kitchen to cook our own meals. Cooking is the last thing I want to do tonight. Two blisters have come up on my baby toes, and I'm feeling mellow and quiet inside. Rather than eat, I head off for bed by 6:30. It's been a day of listening to my inner knowledge and reaping the rewards.

Day 17

Stage 14 - Hornillos del Camino to Castrojeriz
20.2 km (12.55 miles)

Rest was more important than food last night, and I'm feeling much better this morning. My intuition is telling me that today is different. It feels like last night was the last time to share a room with Sheelagh. We never know, if or when, we will see each other again. Adam proved that yesterday. I'm learning to trust my intuition more and more every day, and for whatever reason, this goodbye is different. One of the important lessons I've learned on the Camino is to trust my feelings without needing to know all the answers. It is what it is. Sheelagh has been such an important part of my journey. I'm so grateful that we've spent much of it together. We've laughed, cried and laughed again. But saying goodbye is the right thing to do, so I'm out the door by 6:15.

The doves are cooing "good morning" in the dark. I quickly realize that I don't need my headlamp, so I put it away. It's colder today and a light drizzle is just enough to warrant my poncho. My purple hat holds the poncho out of my face so I can see. It's too hard to take pictures in wet weather. It's not a day of sights; it's a day of sounds.

The cuckoo bird is singing. Its *cuckoo, cuckoo* makes me smile. Which is ironic because cuckoo birds have an unsavory aspect, similar to the Cowbird from Texas. They are brood parasite birds—instead of building their own nest, they lay their eggs in other species' nests. A newly hatched cuckoo actually takes over, maneuvering the other nest eggs onto its back and rolling them out of the nest. The Cowbird is bigger than its nest mates, causing the parents to feed it first, often times, starving their own babies. Knowing the cuckoo's evolutionary survival technique doesn't mean that I can't enjoy its sound. We are all a part of the circle of life, and I'm betting the nest birds are finding ways to battle the nest snatchers.

Both books I read before coming to Spain mentioned a day of boot sucking mud and today is my day. The red dirt feels like glue. I've tried walking in the grass next to the path, but the dirt is humped up on the edge and unsteady to walk on. The sucking mud is safer than a turned ankle. The mud forms a lump under my shoes and grows with each step. My normal turtle pace has become even slower. It's one of those times that it's better to laugh, because it would be so easy to cry.

Just past Hornillos this morning, the trail climbs to a higher mesa, which will drop to a lower mesa in Hontanas. I'm alone on the trail, just me and the mud and strategies for making my way through it. In the distance ahead, several Pilgrims from San Bol join the trail and quickly disappear in the mist.

Between the green earth and gray skies, the only points of interest are the wind turbines in the distance. Coming up is the red exclamation mark symbol in my guidebook indicating a steep descent into Hontanas. The sticky mud turns into wet gravel, creating slick conditions. Picking my way carefully down the hill, I look forward to feeling warm and dry and getting out of my wet shoes and poncho for a while. Despite the rough conditions, I'm happy to complete the 10.8 km walk in 2.5 hours.

Hontanas has several options for a break. Cold and aching, I stop at the first one I see. When I arrive at the café, the small room only has a few patrons. I wait my turn, then soak in the warmth and feel the tension of the road slipping away. As I enjoy my breakfast sandwich, fresh squeezed juice and hot chocolate, I work the kinks out of my feet. I'm in no hurry to leave this haven. I'm already half way to my destination and it's not even 9:00 yet.

But all good things must come to an end, and I won't make it to Castrojeriz sitting in this chair. The drizzle has slowed down enough to snap some interesting photos of the town. The statues and artwork on the Camino have all been different. Most are inspiring, some are confusing. One statue in Hontanas makes me laugh out loud. Someone in this town sure has a sense of humor. Next to an incredible two-story, cut-stone house, with a three-story turret, is the statue of a man taking a leak with a smile on his face. I love it.

Passing through town, I wave to Kris on the front porch of a café and spot Justine and Kate inside. On the other side of town, the path follows a ridge and then drops down to a modern road. The path next to the road is too small to walk on, so I walk on the concrete, staying close to the white line. Good news is that there is little traffic. Bad news is that the drivers seem irritated by Pilgrims clogging the roadway and buzz me as they whiz past.

The Pilgrim traffic has picked up. Taking advantage of the clearing weather and a fellow soul, I ask to have my picture taken in my poncho, rope belt and big smile.

Before this journey I would never have thought I would enjoy walking in the cold rain on a deserted road, and yet, here I am, enjoying the adventure of a lifetime.

Halfway to Castrojeriz, the road passes through the ruins of a convent dating back to 1146. It was built to provide care for Pilgrims and cure victims of a Middle Age disease known as the "Fire of San Anton." I appreciate the signpost written in Spanish and English so that I can better appreciate the significance of the falling ruins.

The tree-lined roadway leads straight towards Castrojeriz. The village sits on top of a dome-shaped mesa—falsely appearing close. The map shows that I have many kilometers left to go and a climb into the city before I can rest today. It would be easy to feel frustrated by how long it takes to reach my destination, but that doesn't serve me. Instead, I change my focus to the details around me and enjoy the green fields of the countryside with its sprinkling of pink flowers. I have no idea what they are, but they look like a cross between a snapdragon and a bluebonnet. In changing my focus, I enjoy where I am instead of longing to be somewhere else. Step by step, I'm closer to my goal. The celebration is in each step, the process, not the destination.

The village looks easy enough to navigate. The map shows a long narrow town with two roads running parallel and a few cross streets. The road I'm on is steep and slick from the drizzle that has returned. Each village and town has a different feel, or vibration, and this one has been accurately described in my guidebook as "permanently occupied with a siesta." I'm fascinated by the contrast in doorways, and wonder what lies behind them. One building has rotten, unpainted wood patched together and held secured by a rock propped at its ragged bottom. Another is a beautifully modern, wooden, carved door with attractive vines growing up stone columns. After my stay in the "exclusive" hotel, I can imagine fantastic interiors behind the doorways.

My goal is to find the Hotel La Posada and pray they have a vacancy. Dennis highly recommends this hotel, but it is small and many people, like Dennis, book their rooms in advance.

What a difference a day makes. Yesterday leaving Burgos, my intuition was directing me like an arrow across the open countryside, and today, in a tiny village, I can't find a single building, or find anyone to ask directions.

Despite my desire for a hot bath and dry clothes, I can't help but stop and appreciate the breathtaking view of the surrounding countryside. That is, until an hour later, lost in this tiny hamlet, I barely miss being run over by a car backing down and around a curve on one of the cross streets. I'm not sure which one of us is more surprised, but he takes off like a rocket while I catch my breath from the near miss.

Despite nearly running me over, I was hoping to ask him how to get to Hotel La Posada. Oh well. I've just about covered the entire town, tromping up and down the cross streets, when I finally find the hotel. Yippee! It takes several minutes to rouse the attention of a staff member, only to learn they are full. Facing the cold, wet weather on aching feet makes me want to cry.

I head back into the rain and pass Dennis coming towards me on a side street. We laugh and make arrangements to meet for dinner. I still have a bed to find, so our conversation is short. This is a small village of 500 people, and I've already walked most of the village. Now I'm one of the LAST ones in town looking for a room.

The Hotel Iacobus is right down the street from La Posada. Although there are no private rooms available, there is a room on the top floor with incredible views with two bunk beds and a private bath, with a BATHTUB! Since no one else is in the room, and it's late, I figure I will have the room to myself.

After a long hot bath, I head down to the restaurant to enjoy a beer and connect to Wi-Fi. The bar is lively with locals and Pilgrims alike. Several framed compostelas decorate the walls. Their stamps are fascinating, because I know each one tells a story.

A fourth wall that's all windows overlooks an empty courtyard. The wet weather has driven everyone inside.

Justine and Kate wander in and we catch up on the day. We only see each other in passing on most days, but Justine's smiling face always provides a lift to my spirit.

The clock says I have time for a nap before dinner with Dennis, so I return to my room. Because I have the room to myself, I've chosen the bottom bunk, closest to the door, and tied my clothes line (poncho belt) from post to post from the upper bunk. I feel like I'm in a tent and enjoy several hours of rest.

Since Pilgrim meals usually aren't served until 7:00, hungry Pilgrims mill around waiting for the doors to open. Often times, strangers meet in line and become friends over a delicious meal. Tonight is no different. Dennis and I are a few minutes early and, while waiting, he introduces me to his friend, Floyd. Floyd also booked all his hotel rooms in advance, and several times on this journey he and Dennis have been at the same hotel on the same night. They are both staying at Hotel La Posada tonight. They remind me of Sheelagh and me, and I send her a prayer.

An Australian couple and Denise from Arizona join us to round out our table of six. Dennis isn't feeling well tonight. His face is pale and sweaty and he picks at his food. He says he'll be OK, but both Floyd and I are worried about him. After dinner, we part ways and I trek back to my hotel, and send Dennis a prayer.

With the seven-hour time difference between Spain and Texas, it's only 2:00 p.m. at home. Unlike yesterday, I have plenty of energy tonight, which is good because I need to talk to Gerald and our office manager, who also happens to be my oldest daughter, Tiffany. I received an ugly text from an unhappy, soon-to-be-ex-tenant. His lease has ended and he's unhappy that I will not renew. Although he has known for six months that he will have to move, and has already found another lot, Gerald's meeting with him today made it real, and he wants me to know what he thinks about me. Not much.

The text message is an uninvited guest, invading my peace and calm. His angry vent needs no response. There's nothing I can say or do to make him feel better. Logic doesn't work with people in the midst of an emotional state. I'm not surprised by his text. Anger has been his go-to response in the past. Intellectually, I understand his opinion of me is untrue, but it still feels like I swallowed a big dose of negativity. Adding to my list of woe, I lost my pen and broke two containers today. I had to throw away my hand sanitizer and the small bottle of bath gel I got from the "exclusive" hotel.

Recognizing the sign of growing negativity, I realize it's time to make a choice. Allow this unwelcome worm to continue to grow or squash it. Gratitude breaks down negativity and is a choice. Gerald and Tiffany will take care of the business while I'm gone, so I remind myself, "Not my circus, not my monkey."

My attitude adjustment comes just in time. The hospitalera knocks on my door at 9:30 asking if I'm comfortable sharing my room with a male bicycle rider. He has just arrived and can't find a place to stay. Without hesitation, I agree to share the room and can't imagine how hard his day has been.

He doesn't speak English and seems uncomfortable sharing the room with me. After a quick shower, he settles into his bunk, pulling the blanket from the top bunk to make his own tent of privacy. It's after 10:00 before we turn out the lights. Lying in the dark, I send prayers for my family at home, as well as my growing Camino family. All is well. I am safe.

Today has been a muddy, suck-your-boots-off kind of day. In walking through the mud, I learned it's not the time to stop, it's the time to keep going. Just like life.

Day 18

Stage 15 - Castrojeriz to Frómista
25.2 km (15.66 miles)

I'm on the road by 6:20. It's not raining, but it's still pretty dark. The path out of town is easy to find and cuts through the green fields surrounding the village. Thick clouds blanket the rising sun, only providing marginal relief to the darkness and hiding the mesa above me. I cross the bridge over the Rio Odrilla and enjoy a concert of birds and frogs greeting the day.

The map shows the trail descending from Castrojeriz, followed by a steep climb to the next mesa. Whoever said the Meseta is flat was lying. The last hill I worried about turned out fine, and according to Dennis, this one is easy as well.

These morning solitary walks are soothing to my soul. It is the first time in my life that I have experienced this quiet time alone with myself and the Creator. Everything feels like magic. Nearing the mesa, I'm stopped short by a sign informing me that I have 1050 meters to climb on a 12% grade. I don't need Gerald's engineering skills to know this hill is a challenge. But one thing I've learned on this journey is that I LOVE challenges. Each time I face one and overcome it, I'm better prepared for the next one. So far, I've been successful, gaining skills on taking care of myself and having a great time doing so.

As I climb, I review my gratitude list. I found my lost pen this morning, yay. Tackling this hill in the early morning, while

I'm fresh, is a Blessing. I'm by myself and don't have to worry about people passing me. The gravel path is soft on my feet. It's not raining yet. The sky is changing with every minute, like a continuous movie of color, from light blue to purple and back to blue. The white clouds on the horizon look like sails blowing across an ocean. Each level of altitude offers a different view of the patchwork quilt of fields below. And, I hear my favorite bird urging me on—*cuckoo, cuckoo.* The list is endless when you focus on being grateful.

By 7:30, I'm eating my breakfast in the lean-to hut at the top of the hill, sheltered from the chilly wind and increasingly wet weather. I can feel the presence of those who have come before me and wonder what the climb was like for them. It's cold and damp enough to warrant putting on rain gear. Something I haven't worn since plodding through the snow over the Pyrenees Mountains.

The vegetation on this high Meseta top clings to the earth, holding on for dear life from the constant wind. Large rocks dot the landscape, and the few trees look to be recently planted. Their thin trunks submit to the force of the wind. It's not a place to linger so I keep moving. By the time I reach the downhill side, the sky has turned to soup, and I'm unable to see the valley below. A warning sign shows an 18% grade for 350 meters. Downhill is more dangerous than uphill, I know, and wonder what the trail will be like on this steep decline in the rain. My map shows the dreaded red exclamation mark again. As I crest the ridge, I'm greatly relieved to discover secure, easy-to-grip concrete on the steep descent. Another item to add to my gratitude list. Reaching the valley, the trail levels out, returning to the soft gravel that is so easy on the knees and feet.

The Camino stretches like a brown ribbon lying on a blanket of green and continues as far as the eye can see. The sky drops down to meet the earth, and I feel like I'm walking through a cloud on a sea of green grass. It is the most beautiful day ever. I'm alone, but never alone. I feel like the honored guest on a personal tour of God's private garden.

Yellow, blue and white flowers speckle the grass with occasional splashes of red. Hulking dark shapes from distant hills serve as a backdrop to the red poppies when I bend down to photograph them from ground level. The road is covered in adorable striped snails crawling their way across the path. With my turtle gait, I empathize with the snail, feeling run over by the faster walkers. I stop to take their picture and step gingerly to avoid crunching them.

At the edge of the valley floor, a rest area with concrete benches has been built to provide a place to rest. Industrious entrepreneurs offer juice, fruit and other snacks to weary Pilgrims. While I'm enjoying a box of juice, Justine arrives without her usual traveling companions. And shortly after her, the lovely French couple joins us. Since we all met on the same night in Larrasoaña, it feels like another reunion. Our joy is contagious and the entrepreneur offers to take our picture together. The couple departs quickly. Justine lingers and joins me for a short break.

This is the first time I've had the pleasure of walking with Justine. Even though we've enjoyed each other's company for several weeks now, there is something special about walking and talking that opens up the heart-to-heart communication lines. We swap stories, discovering mutual interests in St. John Island, Cancun, Mexico and upcoming grandbabies.

With the exception of the rest stop, the landscape is void of human construction until we reach the San Nicolás de Puentetitero Hospital de Perigrinos. This pilgrim hospice was built in the 12th Century next to the river, and retains its rustic charm. There is no electricity in the original structure. Pilgrims enjoy evening meals by candlelight. It's only open from June to September and is limited to providing shelter for twelve Pilgrims at a time. An extension has been added to the main building and provides the modern convenience of showers and toilets.

As we pass, we see that it's open for exploration, which is unusual because it isn't yet open. With the exception of modern bunk beds tucked against the wall, stepping into the building is like stepping through time. The only light entering the front door comes through windows on either end of the rectangular-shaped building. A long table topped with a red tablecloth fills the room. On one end of the building, a wooden staircase leads upstairs. At the other end, stone steps lead to a stone altar area. Soot from candles stain the stone walls above the metal candleholders. The room is filled with the energy of Pilgrims who have received refuge within its walls, providing peace for Justine and I to enjoy.

Outside, sitting on a wooden bench, is a gentleman dressed in all black, including black beret and glasses. The darkness of his clothing stands in sharp contrast to his background of rock wall and rock walkway. He has a trimmed white beard. He looks entirely amused by Life. His eyes and smile radiate kindness and humor. He makes me want to sit down next to him and soak up some of his joy. Instead, I ask if I can take his picture. He nods his approval, and I quickly capture his sweetness in my camera.

After our tour, Justine and I wait to cross the bridge over the Rio Pisuerga, allowing a large bicycle group to go ahead of us.

Like the building we just left, the bridge is as strong today as the day it was built. Crossing the bridge, we leave the Burgos Region and enter the Province of Palencia. Palencia is the land of fields—extensive irrigation systems, few trees and flat, flat land.

We have traveled 9+ km to reach the first village on the route, Itero de la Vega. As we enter the village, we see a picnic area to our left next to an attractive ancient church. The picnic tables are a perfect place to park our backpacks so that we can get out of our rain gear. The sky is still cloudy but the rain has stopped. The temperature is warming from cold to cool, but due to the nature of rain gear, I'm starting to sweat. If I don't get out of this hot suit I will be raining on the inside of my coat.

Entering town, we see a woman talking on the phone standing next to a parked car. As we pass, she hands us a flyer for a local restaurant. Farther down the road, around the bend, several flyers litter the route. I'm saddened by both the marketers for commercializing the Camino and anyone who has disregard for the environment. As a business woman, I understand the need for attracting customers. I also know that if I saw my flyers tossed to the ground I would find a better eco-friendly way to market my business. The current marketing strategy might be damaging their business. Pilgrims like me may actually be boycotting the establishment because of their marketing strategy.

Justine and I stop at the first bar in the village. We enjoy a leisurely breakfast. I work my feet while our story swap continues. At the end of breakfast, Justine thanks me. Confused, I ask why and discover that this is the first time on the Camino that she has taken time to enjoy a cup of coffee without being in a hurry.

After breakfast we follow the trail out of town and enter the "land of the fields." Wind turbines spin in the distance on top of hills. The gray overcast clouds provide drama to the landscape of green fields. Shin-high, green growth blows in the breeze. And although I'm no longer alone, the magic of the countryside continues to sooth my soul. We walk side by side on the wide trail, content, for the most part, to enjoy the scenery in silence.

After eight kilometers, we're both ready to take a break in the next village. Boadilla del Camino is the only opportunity we'll have to stop before making the final 6-km push to Frómista, tonight's destination. I'm not about to pass up either one of my two opportunities to use indoor plumbing on this 25-km day. And, it's time to refuel.

Dennis and Sheelagh have been on my mind today. I'm sending them healing prayers. I've been keeping an eye out for Dennis, but haven't seen him yet. The bar in Boadilla is busy. Justine and I sit outside, which is preferable so that I can work my feet without concern of stinky-feet smell inside. At home, I would feel very out of place taking my shoes off at the table, but here it is critical for my success. Each time I stretch my feet, they rejuvenate and I'm able to continue.

As we're preparing to leave, in walks Dennis. I'm so relieved to know he's feeling better. I didn't realize how concerned I was for him, until I found out he was OK. We briefly discuss hotels and dinner plans for tonight. I'm hoping to copy his playbook and get a room in the same hotel that he's staying in. I just hope I don't spend hours wandering around town to find it. It feels like a race for a bed each night, and speed is not my thing. My aim is to get out of this rat race.

Leaving Dennis behind at the bar, Justine and I return to the Camino. This part of the trail is a wide, tree-lined, gravel path with occasional potholes filled with water from the morning's rain. Cattails grow along the drainage ditches. The weather is perfect for walking. My long-sleeved, wool shirt keeps me warm but breathes.

The path climbs to the Canal de Castilla, where locals join Pilgrims in enjoying strolls in the fresh air. The trail is busier now. I hear the crow's *caw* and the encouraging *cuckoo, cuckoo.* Justine and I discuss plans for finding a bed, and I share my plan to book a room at Dennis' hotel. I predict he'll arrive just in time to lead us to our destination. As if on cue, he shows up exactly as I predicted.

With Dennis in the lead and me bringing up the rear, we cross the canal and are back to concrete. A narrow sidewalk follows the road, hemmed in on both sides by tall concrete walls that starkly contrast the natural beauty of the countryside. No wonder the locals walk next to the canal.

At the top of the hill, we come to a plaza. Dennis has never stayed in this hotel and isn't sure where to go. Oh great, more wandering around town, my feet say. The guidebook doesn't offer a detailed map of Frómista, and the signs are less clear. It's 3:30 and the tourist office is closed for siesta. In our search for a room, we see Phillip and Anne, brother and sister from England, and Kate. They are in search of a pharmacy and groceries for tomorrow's long walk. Justine, Dennis and I are all in need of restocking, so we join the search party for food and supplies.

I can feel a blister forming on my right foot's little toe, so every step is torture. Everyone is exhausted; we look and feel like walking zombies. The pharmacy is closed for siesta, but the grocery store is open. I purchase blister care as well as a handful of supplies for tomorrow. After everyone has made their purchases, we reconvene in the square and make plans to meet for dinner.

Dennis takes the lead in search of our hotel, with Justine and I following him like baby ducks. Thank goodness the town is small and the hotel isn't far away. After some confusion with the hospitalera, Justine and I are able to each secure a private room. Our rooms don't have a private bath like Dennis' room, but we do have our own place to crash. Our rooms come with a sink, but we'll use a shared bathroom for everything else.

The hotel doesn't offer laundry services which I'm in desperate need of. All three pair of underwear, my wool shirt and sports bra are dirty and stinky. Not to be deterred by the lack of services provided, I wash my clothes in the sink in my room and create a clothes line from the closet rod to a chair to dry them. Despite vigorous ringing, they still drip, so I use an extra towel to soak up the drips. My clothes line has proven to be one of the most useful items I've brought, serving double duty as a belt for my poncho on windy rainy days.

I've grown used to wearing my pajamas to dinner. What is *not* normal for me is "going commando." But all three pairs of underwear and both sports bras are drying in my room. A girl has to do what a girl has to do. And besides, I'm the only one who knows. By layering my green shirt over my short-sleeved shirt, I stay warm and it hides the fact that I'm not wearing a bra. The Camino offers all kinds of opportunities to overcome adversity and get creative with what you have, in ways I could never have imagined.

After leaving our respective rooms for the evening, we gather in the square at the appointed time to decide on a place to eat. We're limited in our choices because of the early hour. We're all hungry, tired and ready to fall in bed. After several attempts, we make a choice. Well, not really. It is the only restaurant open that offers an early Pilgrim meal. Our international table companions tonight include Phillip and Anne from England, Dennis, Justine and myself from the United States and Floyd, Kate and Kris from Canada.

Looking for some variety, I order pizza. And beer, of course. Or two. Back home, I'm not normally a beer drinker, but the beer in Spain is delicious, refreshing and flavorful. Pilgrim dinners are relaxed, joyous occasions, and this one is no exception.

As we're leaving the restaurant, I notice other Pilgrims enjoying their dinner. I wave to the French couple, and as I pass a table of two Dutch men, one stops me to ask, "Are you the Texan who soaks her feet in the bidet?" They are the two men I met in the bar in Roncesvalles! After confirming that I am indeed that Texan, they seem shocked and surprised that I've made it this far. I'm amused by their surprise. People who met me early on the trip keep looking surprised when they see me.

Back in my room, I peek beneath the bandages of my sore feet. Both baby toes have tiny blisters on the topsides. I have no idea if I'm treating them properly; I'm no blister expert. After reading the directions on my new blister care, I wrap them up and hope for the best. Despite these new foot issues, my body is holding up remarkably well. Thinking back to the Dutch men's surprise tonight reminds me of the saying, "Don't judge a book by its cover." It is equally true for Pilgrims. It's what's on the inside that counts.

While my body is feeling good, my heart aches tonight. I'm not sure what has triggered these feelings, but I'm missing my husband, Gerald, deeply.

Day 19

Stage 16 - Frómista to Carrión de los Condes
20.5 k (12.74 miles)

This hotel is not Pilgrim friendly. I had an inkling about it yesterday when they didn't provide laundry services, and last night was crazy. I mean CRAAZZYY. The noise from the room next to me lasted until after midnight. The walls are paper thin, and I'm not sure what was going on, but at least four people were involved, two of them children. Earplugs are helpful for snoring but do nothing to faze the high-pitched scream of an unhappy child. I thought about saying something but figured they had enough to contend with; they were doing the best they could, and it was another opportunity for me to accept and surrender.

I wake up late feeling groggy. Rather than wait for the hotel to serve breakfast, I hit the road by 7:20. It's only 3.5 km to the next town of Población de Campos, and it looks like a good place to stop for breakfast. While eating a croissant and juice, I meet another couple that I'd seen at dinner last night, Dale and Becky. They are a nice couple from Seattle and I feel immediately connected to them. It is the same feeling I had when I met Sheelagh and Dennis. Dale reminds me of Gerald—tall, thin, with a gentle spirit. Becky is blonde, trim and equally gentle in spirit. They are the kind of people you instantly like. I feel like I have met two angels.

On most days, Pilgrims have a choice of routes to reach their destination. The Brierley guidebook marks the preferred route with yellow dots, alternative routes with gray dots, optional detours to points of interest in blue dots and alternative scenic routes, like the trip Justine, Mike, Sheelagh and I took to ring the bell in Zabaldica, in green dots.

Today's map shows two routes, and it's time to make a decision. Just after Población de Campos, the preferred route veers to the right before the bridge. The preferred route runs next to the road, straight as an arrow to Carrión de los Condes. The alternative route is a tree-lined, natural path running along the Rio Ucieza for the majority of the day and is slightly longer than the preferred path. With blisters multiplying, I'm not interested in taking any extra steps today, so I choose the preferred route, cross the bridge and commit to a 14-km roadside hike to my destination.

Actually, I'm looking forward to walking next to the road today. The harsh straight lines on the map match the bleakness in my soul, and it gives me an excuse to listen to the iPod shuffle that I purchased in preparation for this trip. For almost three weeks I've carried my iPod, but never listened to it, the sounds of the Camino more interesting than the shuffle's playlist. But today, I'm welcoming the music and counting on it to cover the road noise and sooth my broken heart.

The iPod shuffle is a new addition to my routine and it involves a learning curve. After an experiment or two on placement, I settle on putting the iPod in my shirt pocket, the one with the handy hole on top. What a great idea! After several attempts, I figure out that when I put my hat on first and then the earbuds, I don't get a tangled mess of wires, hat straps and glasses. It seems like a lot to manage. When carrying all your gear all the time, less is more.

Excited about this new experience, I hit the play button and the lyrics from Alabama's "Forever Is As Far As I Will Go" sing in my ears. I burst into tears. Are you kidding me? This is the first song on my playlist? While I'm processing whether to stop, dig the shuffle out of my pocket and hit the next button, the song continues to open my heart. My emotions bubble up. I bawl like a baby. The words from Alabama's song are a message from home. Gerald loves me this way, I know, he loves me forever.

Rather than turn the music off, I let it play. For the next 4 km, I walk and cry, allowing the music to draw my emotions to the surface to be released. Music is powerful. Today, the lyrics connect me to my husband half way around the world and open up an emotional channel that I didn't know was blocked.

Music can be anchored to memories, and hearing a song can bring back that time and place. In January 2005, after my dad's recovery from a bout of pneumonia, and feeling optimistic about his upcoming lung cancer treatment, he wanted to talk about his funeral.

He told me he wanted "Blueberry Hill" by Fats Domino played at his funeral. I'm not sure what memories were attached to the song, but at his funeral, my mom, an Alzheimer's victim, smiled. We played it again, eight months later, at her funeral. Every time I hear it now, I picture my parents dancing in Heaven with dreamy smiles on their faces.

By the time I reach Villarmentero de Campos, I'm emotionally spent, yet amazed at how quickly the time has passed. This trek has been a blur of tears. The café I stop at is different from others I've visited. It reminds me of rural Texas, where industrious folks with no zoning regulations scrounge up some building supplies and slap a room together. The covered "patio" is rectangular and made of raw wood. Two disco ball light fixtures hang from the ceiling. On both of the long sides of the patio, green cloth chairs, connected like movie theater seats, face each other. In between them is a green, painted, wooden table, with two red ashtrays sitting on top. And then there are the ducks. And green globs of duck poo haphazardly scattered on the concrete floor.

I'm relieved to have a place to sit, enjoy a cup of hot chocolate, a cup of fresh squeezed orange juice and tend to my feet. The poo doesn't bother me. As a horsewoman, I'm accustomed to worse. Actually, it makes me feel better for what I'm about to do. A new blister on my big toe needs to be drained. With socks and shoes removed, needle and thread ready, I realize that I've left my scissors in my backpack, across the room. Before I can decide if I'm going to tip toe around the green poo, or put my socks and shoes back on to reach my backpack, Dale and Becky, my new Camino angels, walk in. I'm so relieved to see them and ask for help. In addition to getting my scissors, Becky has Betadine to sanitize my needle. Hmmm, Betadine, that's a good idea. I will purchase some at the next opportunity.

I snatch a photo of a Korean Pilgrim who is following the ducks around the yard to take their picture. A few minutes later, one of the ducks walks right up to me and tries to snap my baby toe. He is so close, I can't resist taking his picture before protecting my feet. The ducks are a delightful relief to this morning's storm of emotions.

Before leaving, I call the same hotel that Dennis will be staying at in Carrión to book a room. I don't have to worry about speed when I can book in advance. For me, it's the best way to avoid the rat race when I reach the town where I plan to sleep.

Dale and Becky are headed to Carrión as well, but they don't have reservations yet. We say goodbye and I leave them to enjoy the remainder of their rest stop.

I've had enough emotion for the day, so I put the shuffle in my belly pack and enjoy the comforting sounds of the Camino. I wave to the French couple as I pass by Villalcázar de Sirga. Normally, I wouldn't pass up a bathroom break, but I'm on a mission today. On this flat land, you can see forever and my destination lies ahead. It's only 1:30 when I reach Carrión de los Condes. The Pilgrim statue at the edge of town welcomes me.

From here I can see my hotel. No wandering around town today! A gated entrance leads to a private courtyard with three round concrete tables and benches. The potted plants break up the monotone color of the stone exterior and patio. Red archways add a splash of color. Inside my room, a full bed covered in a bright pink bedspread takes up the majority of the space. The bathroom has a bathtub, which makes me happy. I can see why Dennis has booked this place for two nights. Its villa-like atmosphere is a peaceful place to spend a rest day.

The Facebook posts and photos have been easy to share, until today. I'm always conscious about what I'm sharing and why. My purpose is to inspire others and let my family know where I am and that I'm doing well. What, if anything, do I share about today? I don't want my friends and family to be concerned about me. They know I don't cry often. But, to not share the experience feels like I'm hiding the truth, that I'm keeping a secret. And I know, from Brené Brown's book, *The Gifts of Imperfection*, that shame hides in secret places. Growing up, I was told big girls don't cry. But they do. I certainly did today. There is no shame in crying. I'm willing to be vulnerable and real, so I post about my crying day.

The Camino isn't the miles you walk; it's the miracles you experience. It's a short story about life, providing lessons that could otherwise take a lifetime to learn. It's the continuous connection with people you meet, people that touch your heart. Sheelagh, Dennis, the French couple, Adam, Justine, Phillip and Anne, and now, today, I'm adding my angels, Dale and Becky, to my growing list. The 500-mile trek is the vehicle for the connections, and I'm excited to see what each day brings, celebrating each connection as it occurs.

I'm grateful to the Dutch men for reminding me of who I am— the Texan who soaks her feet in the bidet. I'm not embarrassed about doing whatever it takes to complete this journey with Ease and Grace. The Camino has been the perfect testing ground for my GRIPP Life™ philosophy. It is important to prove to myself that my ideas work. Thanks to the Camino, the feedback has been instantaneous.

Today's feedback is "Get some rest, girl." My feet are manufacturing blisters, and I'm exhausted, emotionally and physically. Following Dennis' lead, I book my room for another night in this paradise. I'm heeding the advice from my internal guidance system and giving myself permission to rest.

After a hot bath, I head out to find a pharmacy to stock up on some Betadine. It seems like a good idea to have some in my pack. According to the sign, the store should be open, but it's Sunday in Spain. Business hours are iffy, at best, and the pharmacy isn't open yet. The rain has returned, so I dart into a local bar. And, for the third time in one day, I see Dale and Becky.

We chat over a beer and a snack and talk about the day. They're headed to a church service in a few minutes and invite me to join them, but I decline. I prefer to spend the time relaxing, writing my daily notes and enjoying the ambiance of the town. We make plans to eat together after the service.

Dinner with Dale and Becky is delightful. They are both good listeners and wise, kind people. Talking with them helps me process my crying day, and I make them laugh. They aren't taking a rest day tomorrow and travel at a fast pace. I don't know if I will see them again, but I hope so. We exchange telephone numbers to communicate on WhatsApp and say goodnight. A strong friendship was born in a single day.

When I return to the hotel, I run into Justine and Dennis. Justine has booked a room here as well, and the three of us share the same courtyard. Over a glass of wine, we talk about the day, laugh about the crazy noise last night and call it a day. My crying day is over and I'm ready for a good night's sleep.

Email to Richard:

I haven't heard from you in several days. You OK?

Love from Carrión de los Condes

Square in Carrión de los Condes

Day 20

Rest Day in Carrión de los Condes

My morning started with a breakfast connection with Tanja, my roommate in Estella. Seeing her makes me realize that she's on my list of special people too. Her infectious smile and sincere happiness to see me always make me feel loved. After breakfast, she braves the rain and cold to continue her journey while I enjoy a cup of hot chocolate and contemplate what I'll do today.

First on the agenda is a shopping trip to the Pilgrim store. These stores cater to Pilgrims and carry everything from walking supplies to souvenirs. Most towns don't have a store like this; Carrión has two or three. I'm on the hunt for a second pair of new tips for my walking poles. I bought a pair of rubber tips in Pamplona and they are already worn out. The *click, click, click* gets old after a while.

Dennis and I are shopping together. He's looking for postcards. Sending postcards while walking the Camino wasn't on my list of things that I had considered, until today. This gift of time has made it possible, so I purchase ten cards to send to family and friends. Our next stop is the tobacco store to purchase stamps. Who knew? Dennis does and I am so grateful for his mentorship.

Our next stop is the bank ATM. I don't use them at home, much less when the instructions are written in Spanish. With

Dennis' help, I'm able to restock my cash. Touring the town in the rain and cold isn't much fun, so we return to the hotel. After making plans to meet for dinner, we go our separate ways.

My afternoon is all about hot baths (three), naps (two), writing postcards (ten), and conversations with family (three). Gerald and I talk on the phone. The conversations with my daughters are by text. Both girls are facing challenging situations at home with houses right now.

Tiffany's house had a water leak. Her husband, almost two-year-old daughter and she are living in a suites hotel while their house is being rebuilt. Oh, and she is very pregnant, her second daughter due in June. As for my other daughter, Brittany's house is days away from closing. Now her buyer is backing out of the contract. Both girls are missing their momma. And I'm missing my family.

Between baths, naps, writing and texting, I replace the new tips on my poles, clean my gums under the flap cover, and dry my socks with the hairdryer by placing them over the end of the dryer. The hot air blows the sock up and they dry quickly. It is so wet and cold today, I'm afraid my socks won't be dry tomorrow. What a great day to take a break. I'm so glad I'm not walking in this weather. It is by far the worst weather day yet.

It's hard to not walk after spending so many hours on the road every day, even if it is cold and wet. After a delicious dinner with Dennis, I take a stroll around town by myself. The rain has slowed down. The streets are almost empty. I find my way to the Rio Carrión and watch the water flow. I really appreciate the beauty. It's not something we get to see very often in my drought-stricken, Hill Country home.

As I'm wandering around town, I meet three new women. During our conversation, I discover that one swears she is blister free because she wears knee-high half-hose under her socks. Desperate to stop the proliferation of blisters, I hustle to the grocery store and buy a pair to try tomorrow.

On the way back, I visit the church across from the hotel. No one else is inside and I'm able to take my time and enjoy the beauty of the church. Candles are available for sale, on the honor system, and I purchase two and light them for my girls.

Back in my room, I'm ready for bed, but not exhausted. I really needed this day of rest and feel great about the decision to take a day off. Thank you, Lord, the pain has left my toes. I'm feeling supported by the new moon tonight. I'm rip snortin' and ready for tomorrow.

A beautiful park in Carrión

Day 21

Stage 17 - Carrión de los Condes to Terradillos de Templarios 26.8 km (16.6 miles)

This hotel is very Pilgrim friendly. Breakfast starts at 6:00 a.m., which is unusual on the Camino. Before the sun is fully awake, I'm fed, packed and out the door, and it's barely 7:00. Under my wool socks, I'm wearing hose as an experiment for the prevention of blisters. A rest day and fresh dressing is all I know to do for the ones I already have, but I'm hoping that the Pilgrim I met last night is correct and the hose will prevent new ones. It's going to be a long day.

Today's goal is Terradillos de los Templarios, a 26.8-km hike, because that is where Dennis is headed. If I were being honest with myself, I'd admit that I AM stalking him. His months and months of research to pick the best lodging is worthy of emulating. During my time on the Camino, I'm paying attention to what works for me and what doesn't. I've learned that a good night's rest has been rejuvenating, making the arduous task of walking enjoyable. Dennis is generous and seems to enjoy my company. The Camino is extraordinary in its ability to form strong bonds in a short amount of time, and the more we talk, the more connections we discover. We have so many things in common, we never run out of subjects. I suspect our friendship will continue after this journey is done.

The first village, Caldadilla de la Cueza, is almost 15 km away, and the only services available are occasional picnic benches. I'm carrying food and a full, heavy water platypus. There will be no fonts, no bathrooms, no bars or cafés for the first half the day. With three weeks of experience under my belt, it's *no problemo*.

I'm amazed by my confidence in tackling today's journey. Growth can happen fast. Sometimes so quickly you don't realize how much, until you compare the current state to a previous state. The progress I've made in the past three weeks is nothing short of miraculous. What a gift this journey has been, and I know it will continue to be. All I have to do is be willing to take the next right step, trust the process and enjoy the journey.

Compared to other mornings, there are more Pilgrims out early today. Some are talking, their voices penetrating through the quiet of the day. Rather than listen to them chat, I tentatively plug in my earbuds and turn on my music. I don't feel the need to cry and am relieved that a rest day is the cure for my crying day. Kahlil Gibran, the famous artist and poet, spoke of the power of music when he said, "Music is the language of the spirit." When my spirit was broken, the music put me in touch with my pain, and produced healing tears. Today, my spirit is filled with adventure and optimism. The music takes me into the artist's world of rhythm, beat and lyrics. Rhythm and beat that kicks up my pace to tackle the strong headwind. The lyrics take me wherever the artist wants me to go.

Since I bought the iPod right before the trip, I was too short on time to build a playlist of my favorite songs. Instead, I created a quick list of favorite artists and figured if a song came on that I didn't care for, I could just skip it. Now that I'm here, listening to the music, I'm glad that I didn't take the time to cherry pick my favorites, because my playlist is filled with surprises, songs that I haven't heard in a long time.

When Randy Travis' song "The Box" came on, I was unprepared. The lyrics tell the story of a son finding his father's box of treasures after he has passed. The dusty box is filled with items that his father treasured and reveals his love that had been kept hidden. I've played the song over and over again, listening closely to the words.

It's been a decade since my parents passed, and I'm still sifting through their stuff. I have questions about a sweet ring that I suspect was Mom's first wedding ring, but will never know for sure. And, what do I do with Dad's Mason's apron? He wanted to be buried with it, but didn't tell us where it was or what it looked like. I found it months after the funeral. I couldn't bring myself to throw it away. None of my brothers wanted it, so it still sits in my closet.

"The Box" reminds me of why I'm walking the Camino. Not only is it an experience of a lifetime, a treasured memory to place inside my own box, it has been a teacher. Each "chance" encounter is an opportunity to show how much we care for each other. In the moment, when it happens. The Camino has been magical in honing this skill with my growing list of Camino Angels. Thank you, Randy Travis, for your unexpected gift to my soul.

After 17 km, Caldadilla de la Cueza is a sight for sore eyes

Between Carrión and Terradillos, I see Dennis twice today. The first time, we pass at the picnic area. I'm leaving after a foot massage, sock change and snack, and Dennis is arriving. The second time, in the darkened entryway of a store in Caldadilla de la Cueza, we both burst out laughing when we see each other. Unlike the picnic area, Dennis couldn't see me before making the decision to stop here for a break. I had debated other stores in the village before choosing this one. The odds of us picking the same place to stop at the same time are pretty staggering, and our joint laughter acknowledges the miracle in the moment.

Dennis' pace is faster than mine, so we say goodbye again. We're mutually respectful for our enjoyment of solitude and Camino pace. He is the hare, I am the tortoise. I'm happy to hear the *cuckoo* over the sound of my music as I trudge down the road. In Ledigos, I learn a few lessons. One, hose does *not* prevent blisters, darn it. Two, Dennis was right. During our break together, he said we had another 10 km to go before the end of the day. And I, misreading my guidebook, had argued with him, that we only had 5 km to go. Bless Dennis, he didn't argue back, even though he knew he was right. He allowed me the privilege of discovering the distance on my own accord.

The other lessons today came from a total stranger. Sitting on a bench on the side of the road, draining my new blister with a needle, an American ex-military Pilgrim stopped to offer assistance. After picking up my pack to check the weight, he offered the following words of wisdom: "Your pack is too heavy. You need to get rid of some weight. This blister is from not resting enough," and "it's not how far you go, it's how far you go after you want to quit." His words gave me the energy to keep moving and more to think about. I still had another 3 km to go, and I was exhausted. He told me exactly what I needed to hear to complete my journey with renewed strength. I made the final 3 km in an hour.

The alburgue is located on this side of the village. From a distance, I can read the large yellow sign on the side of the building, telling me I have arrived, even though I have a ways to go. It is a big, single-story building surrounded by a fenced green pasture. The roof is outlined by bright blue sky. I stagger past empty porch chairs and into the lobby. The bar area is filled with Pilgrims relaxing in the protection of the warm yellow walls. The brisk wind has driven everyone inside on this blustery day.

The hospitalera gives me the good news that a private room is available. Her kindness is palpable and sooths my hurting body and soul. The alburgue provides laundry services at a reasonable cost, and encouraged by my greeting, I'm confident my clothes will be washed and dried without any trouble. Hand washing clothes just doesn't do as well. In my exhaustion, I'm not prepared to fight the cold wind to hang them outside.

After a quick wash in the tiniest shower stall, I put on my night clothes, deliver my dirty clothes to the front desk and enjoy a cold beer while catching up on my daily notes and looking at my guidebook. I know Thom and Jodi are coming soon. It's time to look ahead and make some calculations on how far I need to go each day and make final arrangements for meeting up. At this rate, I'm confident I can make the stage walks outlined in my guidebook, and compare it to Dennis' reservations to see how they match up.

In the midst of my research, Sheelagh blows through the door like a breath of fresh air. I'm overjoyed to see her and relieved to know her ankle hasn't stopped her progress. Like me, she's exhausted and looking for a place to crash for the night. I would offer to split the cost of my room with her, but my room has only one small bed. Since the rest of the private rooms are booked, Sheelagh takes a bed on the alburgue side of the hostel. We make plans to enjoy the 7:00 Pilgrim meal, so that she can get settled in for the night.

By 6:00 p.m., I'm back in the bar and it's hopping with activity. I'm fascinated by the interweaving of people we meet on the Camino and the joy that we're able to share each time we reconnect. Dennis is catching up with a couple from Spain whom he has seen many times. The wife, Anita, is wearing socks and men's sandals that she purchased on the trail so that she can keep going. I take a picture of her shoes, just in case my blisters continue to multiply. I will have an option to pursue so that I can keep going.

Anita is a master storyteller and has us in stitches. My favorite story she told was about a night in an alburgue. She heard moaning from the bunk next to her, did her best to not look, but failed. A Korean husband had slipped down to his wife's bunk in the middle of the night. Anita could hear the zipper on the bedroll open, and the sound of rustling, followed by moaning. Despite her best attempt, she couldn't help but peek, and was surprised to see the husband massaging and exercising his poor wife's legs. There was no midnight tryst, just moans of relief from the rigors of the Camino. Anita had us all wiping away tears of laughter.

Sheelagh and Dennis

Today has certainly been a day of miracles. Because I took a day of rest and Sheelagh has recovered, we're together tonight. Both Sheelagh and Dennis are with me at the same time, and we're enjoying this wonderful meal. New Pilgrims continue to come into my life, sharing their stories and creating new ones. And in the deep recesses of my brain, the words of wisdom I heard in Ledigos are rattling around. What am I going to do about these pesky blisters? I don't want them to look like Anita's feet, which, according to Dennis, look like they went through a meat grinder. I go to bed, praying that my feet heal overnight, and wonder, *Should I let something go?*

Email to Richard:

Made 26.8 km today in a head wind! This is supposed to be the "boring" flat part of the trip, but I have found it delightful.

Did you know the cuckoo bird is real? Every morning for almost a week, I can hear the cuckoo birds. They really sound like the clocks! Makes me laugh.

Feet hurting pretty good, but I'm still moving.

Love you!

Day 22

Stage 18 - Terradillos de Templarios to Bercianos del Real Camino
23.1 km (16.6 miles)

Last night, before going to bed, I turned up the temperature on the old-fashioned water heater to combat the cold. When it didn't respond, I turned it up again. Shivering, I went to bed, hoping that the blankets would trap my body heat and keep me warm during the night. Little did I know, water heaters need a little time to heat up, and I woke up at 12:15, 3:15, and 5:15, sweating like a river from the heat wave I had created. At 6:00 a.m., I give up the idea of sleep and begin preparing for the day.

My guidebook shows another long day, but there are several opportunities to eat, rest and use indoor facilities on this stretch. After dressing my blisters, I wonder about yesterday's question, "Should I let something go?" The hose experiment failed, so it's time to try something new. What can I let go of to lighten my pack?

I begin by drinking the last of the three juice boxes I purchased in Carrion. Not only will it lighten my load, it will give me much needed energy for the day. But, drinking the juice is not the same thing as letting something go. Letting go means leaving something behind, hopefully to the benefit of someone else. In most alburgues, left behind items are placed in a Pilgrim box, recycled to Pilgrims in need of that particular item.

What can I leave behind? The first item that comes to

mind is the Pilgrim cream that the Nashville couple gave me in Roncesvalles. It was a gift, which makes it both easy and hard to leave. Easy, because it hasn't been helpful in preventing blisters, and I didn't make an investment in its acquisition. Energetically, it's the reason why pet shelters make you pay to adopt a pet. From experience, they know that if you have some skin in the game you are more apt to take good care of your new pet. Hard, because the cream was a gift, and to leave it behind feels like I'm dishonoring the love behind the act of giving. And then I realize her gift wasn't the cream, it was her sincere desire to help. If leaving the cream behind helps me today, her act of kindness has been fulfilled. Perhaps not as she had imagined, but helped none the less. With appreciation, I leave the cream on the nightstand without guilt, hoping it will help someone else. I am practicing letting go by lightening my load.

By 6:40, I'm ready to go, but find myself locked inside the building, AGAIN. The door from my hallway into the main part of the alburgue is locked. There is another door at the end of the hallway leading outside, but I'm hesitant to use it. Unlike the medieval casa rural in Viskarret, this is a modern building, with safety-latch doors. And alarms. Before I can make up my mind to open the door, I'm joined in the hallway by Anita and her husband. They're ready to go as well but need to find a way to put their bags on the front porch so that the bag service can pick them up and take them to tonight's destination. By shipping her bag instead of carrying it, Anita has been able to continue her Camino. It only costs a few euros, and from what Anita says, it has made all the difference. Taking stock of the situation, Anita has no hesitation on opening the door to the outside, alarms be damned. I'm not sure if it is a fake alarm, a silent alarm, or one that only rings in the hospitalera's room, but whatever it is, I'm relieved to hear nothing but silence. I'm grateful for Anita's boldness in executing our escape.

While Anita and her husband put their bags on the porch, I hobble out the door and head down the trail. The morning is my favorite time to be alone and gives me time to warm up my feet. They still hurt every morning, but with time and miles, eventually feel better. As I'm saying a prayer for Ease and Grace for today's journey, I hear the *caw* of a crow. It sounds as if it's confirming receipt of my prayer by the Universe.

I can't help but stop to photograph the bright orange flowers growing next to the trail. Although several Pilgrims are on the road, I don't know any of them. A nod of greeting is all it takes to be friendly and maintain my silence. I love the silence. It allows me to listen for the Creator and hear the sounds that surround me. The moon is a bright dot, encircled by a purple inky sky, shining brightly over the broad flat green fields. It is barely light enough to make out the trees lining the trails. My feet have warmed up, and between the silence and the sky, I'm poetry in motion, enveloped by peace and calm.

After crossing the Rio Templarios, the path turns into a concrete roadway for a short distance. From the darkness, I'm surprised to see the outline of a commercial solar panel array so close to the road, and I'm fascinated by the presence of this modern technology on the Camino. I suspect I'm in the minority, based on the non-reactions of my fellow Pilgrims, who pass by without a glance. I'm captivated by the structure and ponder how many people benefit from the solar panels and its impact on their lives. The Camino is an opportunity to see beauty in everything, modern and ancient, natural and manmade, and I look for connections to each of them.

Entering Moratinos, I can't believe my eyes. There is a collection of openings on the side of a hill that look like underground houses. My guidebook makes no mention of them, and I wonder what is hidden under the mound of dirt. I stop to take their picture, and from behind me, I hear my name. Turning around, I see the always smiling faces of Baly and Jose. It has been quite a while since we've seen each other, and I'm happy to walk with them to the next town.

We only have a short time to enjoy each other's company. They've already eaten, but I'm due for a breakfast break. We say *adios*, again. After a delicious cheese sandwich and hot chocolate, I'm ready to tackle the next stage of my journey, a 6-km walk to Sahagún. Today is a series of route choices, one after the other. But basically, it comes down to natural path or roadside walking. For this first choice, I choose the natural path and am rewarded by views of additional earthen houses surrounded by green fields of some kind of grass. I don't know if it's wheat or oats, but it's alive in a way I've never experienced before. The grass stalks glow in the morning sun and gently undulate in the breeze. My phone video camera isn't up to the job of capturing the moment, so I settle for a photo and imprint the experience in my heart and soul.

Nearing Sahagún, the path has some ups and downs to it. On the rises, I can see Dennis ahead of me, his telltale socks swinging from his maroon backpack. I'm ready for some company, so I pick up my pace in hopes to catch him before he reaches the city limits. Dennis wears earbuds to listen to his music while he walks, so I know I'll have to catch up to him to get his attention.

At the second choice point of routes, I follow Dennis on the roadway route and realize I don't have much time to catch him, or I'll lose him in the twists and turns of the city. Rise after rise, I can see that I'm gaining on him, but I can also see the outline of buildings on the horizon. Just as I'm about to give up, on the last rise I catch up to him. Dennis has stopped, back to the path, hidden in the branches of a tree. On the Camino, it's not unusual to see a man with his back to the path, or a woman, typically several steps off the path, squatting down next to a bush. It is the norm on the Camino, and it's polite to look the other way and keep on walking. In this instance, I look the other way and adjust my pace to pass my friend after he has completed his business.

I'm elated to catch him and share my chase story, to his amusement. I don't assume my company is welcome. It's good manners to ask fellow Pilgrims if they want company, but Dennis assures me that my presence is welcome, so we continue together.

In Sahagún, Dennis is ready for his breakfast stop, and although I'm not hungry, my feet can always use a break. Rather than stopping in a bar along the Camino route, Dennis seeks out a restaurant that provides tables and chairs, table cloths and a nice atmosphere. The Camino is a difficult journey of distance and endurance. The accepted norm is to suffer. This man is teaching me to enjoy the journey; he is the epitome of Ease and Grace. I am grateful and inspired by his example of self-care.

Our discussion centers on León and the next few days' schedule. Since we first met, Dennis has urged me to follow his example of bussing through an entire stage of concrete walking. Tomorrow he'll travel 55 km in one day. His plan is to walk 28.4 km to Mansilla de las Mulas, bus 18.1 km to León, and take a cab another 8.5 km to La Virgen del Camino. He is skipping León altogether. He spent time in León on his prior Camino and doesn't feel the need to visit it again.

Despite my trust in his planning and experience, I know I must follow my heart and walk my Camino *my way*. For me, that means enjoying the experience of León. While I still haven't made up my mind about the bus, I do know I want to reserve a private room in the hotel that Dennis has booked tonight in the tiny village of Bercianos del Real Camino. My guidebook shows limited options tonight, and after my sleepless night last night, I'm really looking forward to a room for myself.

Our waiter has been very kind, so I take a risk and ask if he will make a reservation for me at the Hostal Rivero. In addition to the number of beds, rooms and types of lodging, the guidebook provides the telephone numbers for each one. My angel waiter is happy to help, and after the call, I'm ecstatic to discover that I just snagged the last private room at the hotel. Yay! No longer in a race for a bed, I can enjoy the rest of my day confident in my private lodging tonight.

Walking through a herd of sheep

Dennis and I continue to walk together for the rest of the day. We reach the hotel by 1:30 in the afternoon. After waiting our turn to check-in, the hospitalera asks me if I want to share my room with another female Pilgrim who is injured. From what I can tell, with my limited understanding of Spanish, there are two rooms, one with three beds and my private room. The injured Pilgrim is willing to share the cost of the room with three beds. I decide to take the room to myself, figuring that another Pilgrim will be willing to share the room with three beds. My heart is set on some alone time, so I request my private room, much to the obvious disapproval of the hospitalera.

When I unlock my door, I understand the hospitalera's displeasure. There are not two rooms. My "private" room has three beds. By insisting on having the room to myself, the injured woman won't have a place to say tonight in this village. Now that I understand the situation accurately, I welcome the opportunity to help my fellow pilgrim. Horrified, I stagger back down the stairs as fast as I can to correct the situation.

Anita and her husband are in the bar, checking in. I'm happy to see them, knowing that laughter will accompany dinner again tonight, but for now, I ask Anita's husband, a native Spaniard, to help me rectify the situation with my room. Even with his fluent Spanish, he has difficulty communicating with the hospitalera, who is a native of Portugal. Ahh, Spanish is her second language, which is why we are having so much trouble. It takes time, but eventually, we come to an understanding. The hospitalera looks happy now and introduces me to Anne.

Anne is from France but speaks perfect English. This is her sixth year to spend time on the Camino, and she has yet to reach Santiago. She isn't alone in this practice. Others I've met, like Anita and her husband, live in Europe and spend their annual holiday walking as far as they can go each year. The next year, they pick up where they left off from the previous year and continue on their way. There are unlimited ways to walk the Camino.

Anne tore her calf muscle in Sahagún four or five days ago and has been recovering there until today. This is her first day to walk with her injury and she's made it 10 km. Her plan is to continue at this pace until her vacation time is over. For Anne, it's not about the distance, it's about the experience. She loves the Camino lifestyle and living in the moment. She is grateful for the shared room and is understanding about the earlier misunderstanding.

After a quick shower in the community bathroom and a nap, I text Gerald that I've arrived for the day. There is no Wi-Fi, so I'm unable to email Richard. After cleaning my gum's flap cover and draining the fluid from my blister, I head down to the patio to hang my laundry to dry. Sitting in the warm sun, drinking a cold beer, I write in my daily journal. Today, I almost missed the opportunity to be an angel for Anne. Had I known the facts, I would not have hesitated to say yes. When I had clarity on the situation, it was an easy decision to make.

Clarity. How do I reach clarity on riding the bus tomorrow? My feet are begging me to ride. Now that I have experience in walking on concrete, I can see why Dennis is a proponent of skipping it when you can. Perhaps I should be asking the question, "Why not ride the bus?" When I realize that my number one reason for not riding the bus is fear—fear of being judged as "not a real Pilgrim"—I get mad. Mad at myself for caring what other people think, and mad that we humans are so quick to judge each other. With this clarity, I make the decision to ride the bus with Dennis tomorrow, and I feel great about my decision. Not only will I ride the bus, I will share it on Facebook in the hopes of breaking the accepted norm, making it easier for others to do the same. A picture of the sign that hung in my high school stairway flashes before my eyes: "If you are not a part of the solution, you are a part of the problem."

Dinner is as I expected it to be, filled with laughter and the joy of being together. It's colder than it has been in the past, so I'm wearing my waterproof pants over my yoga pants. Our Pilgrim meal consists of beans, beef stew and Santiago almond cake. Yum. Thank you, Creator, for this day of Ease and Grace and the opportunity to be an Angel.

Day 23

Stages 18, 19 & 20 - Bercianos del Real Camino to León
Total 44.5 km (27.6 miles): walking, 26.4 km (16.4 miles),
bus, 18.1 km (11.25 miles)

Before going to bed last night, I warned Anne that if she saw my legs up in the air, swinging from side to side, I was stretching the kinks out, and I expressed my desire to not disturb her. At one point, I know we made eye contact, but can't remember if it was at the 3:00 a.m., 4:00, or 5:15 session. By 5:45, I give up on trying to sleep and start my morning routine. I have an hour until it's time to meet Dennis. For him, 6:45 is an early start, but for me, it is just another day.

The plan is to walk to Mansilla and then ride the bus to León together then part ways. Dennis will cab to La Virgen del Camino, and I will find a place to spend the night in León. I don't have reservations yet, but have Faith that I will find the right place to stay.

Since our first opportunity for breakfast is almost 8 km away, I slurp down a juice box and eat a handful of nuts. Anne is awake but plans to go back to sleep after I leave. The hour passes quickly. My plan to use indoor plumbing is operating beautifully. Today, of all days, is not the day for my plan to fail. It will be a long day, with only two available stops, and the first time to walk all day with Dennis. After rolling my feet and getting dressed, it's time to pack my bag. I have challenged myself to let go of another item this morning. From experience I know daily practices build new habits. Therefore, today, I'm leaving my pink flip flops. They are my shower shoes, but since I'm not staying in alburgues, they're no longer a necessity. If I'm faced with an unsanitary looking shower, I can always use my crocs. No matter how small, it feels good to lighten my load.

After a Buen Camino to Anne, I'm set to go. Dennis is ready when I knock on his door. As quietly as possible, wearing heavy backpacks and carrying walking sticks, we tiptoe down the stairs like a pair of rhinoceroses, find a door that opens to the outside and step into the pre-dawn light. We're greeted by the familiar sound of the crow, and I thank the Creator for the day.

The trail is not wide enough for us both, so I take the lead, set the pace, quickly leaving the tiny village behind us. As the night gives way to the day, rays of sunlight stream through a single break in the clouds that blanket the horizon. The Camino cuts a straight line through the green fields and leads us directly to El Burgo Ranero, a small village of 790 people. A pair of Pilgrims occupy one of the green tables sitting in front of the Cafeteria El Camino. Down the street, in a gentle curve of the road, the church steeple towers above its surroundings, circled by chattering storks.

After dropping our backpacks, we race inside the cafeteria, pleasantly surprised to discover we won't have to decide who gets to go first, because side by side, this bar has both a men's and women's bathroom. In my rush, I fail to notice the last one to use my bathroom has left me stranded. This is not a drip dry situation. Knowing Dennis is next door, I whisper/shout, "Dennis." "Dennis." "Dennis." Gradually, increasing the volume, until I have his attention. "Do you have any toilet paper in your bathroom? Can you hand me some?" We are both laughing as I open the door just wide enough for my Camino angel's hand to deliver the goods.

I'm not sure what I would have done had he not been there, and I'm grateful I didn't have to find out. Realizing the men's room is now without paper, and the women's only has this partial roll, I decide to do my good deed for the day and replenish both bathrooms with paper. After waiting in line behind people ordering their breakfast, the owner looks relieved by my offer to help. These small village cafés often have one person doing all the work, taking orders, cooking the food, squeezing the juice and making coffee. Her smile of gratitude in the midst of the morning rush makes me happy. Such a simple act helps so many people.

We're now facing the longest haul of the day, 12.7 km to Reliegos, traveling a straight, flat, tree-lined trail next to the roadway. The road isn't busy, more like walking on a deserted country road. Pilgrims are ahead of us and behind us, each clump marching to the beat of their own drummers. Dennis and I cue our music and become walking machines.

At the second picnic table area, halfway to Reliegos, we stop for a sock change and a rest. The picnic area is fifteen or so yards from the trail, with lush overgrown landscape. The ground is damp, which makes changing socks a bit challenging. While I roll my feet carefully on my ball so I don't have to chase it barefoot across the mud, Dennis reviews his guidebook.

Gathering our things, we slip back in to the steady stream of Pilgrims heading towards Reliegos. It is a perfect day for a long walk. The walking seems effortless today, a walking meditation, with clear skies, calm winds, unending green fields, smooth gravel trails, and quiet companionship of a good friend. I have turned my music off to absorb the sounds of the Camino. It feels like I can hear through my heart and feet. They are waiting to hear from the Creator. All I have to do is keep walking. The answers will flow in time.

The ecosystem on this portion of the Camino is different. The vegetation next to the trail is waist-high grass dotted with flowers. As we walk, I keep hearing a strange rustling in the grass. I don't know if it's a bird or some other creature, so I keep my eyes peeled hoping to discover what's scrambling in the bushes. While stopped for a water break, a foot-long, green lizard darts into the open. Mystery solved.

Today is the first day that I've seen a lizard on the Camino. From the sounds of the rustling in the bushes, there are plenty of them. How strange that they would show up today, and so often. I'm curious about the symbolism of the lizard and will contact Kim, my friend back home, to check her animal spirit guide. She has already sent me information on the crow and the cuckoo bird. It will be interesting to see what her book says about the lizard.

The walking is effortless, but relentless. It seems like we've been walking forever, but we haven't arrived yet. We stop to check the map and realize Dennis left his guidebook on the picnic bench. He has a different guidebook, but it's not as good as the one he lost. I offer to wait for him to retrieve it, too tired to go with him, but he is willing to let it go.

Entering Reliegos, I smile at the sound of the cuckoo bird welcoming me to town. During our snack stop, I enjoy a beer and croissant. I catch up with Camino Richard, who I met at Orrison along with his friends. He tells me that Baly and Jose are in Mansilla waiting on the bus. I mention that I'm looking for a hotel in León. A Pilgrim I've never met suggests the Parador San Marcos. He says the Parador is like a museum and offers a special Pilgrim rate. According to Richard, Baly and Jose are headed there as well.

Dennis informs me that we need to get going to catch the bus. We have another 2 km to go before reaching Mansilla. With Dennis in the lead, we walk directly to the bus station and arrive at 2:12 and see Baly and Jose. They've been waiting for more than two hours. Dennis and I barely have time to stow our backpacks on the bus. By 2:20, everyone is loaded and we are on our way. Now, that's what I call Ease and Grace!

Forty-five minutes later we arrive in León. Dennis departs in his cab, and Baly and Jose graciously invite me to share their cab to the Parador. Seeing the hotel, I remember it from *The Way*. The rate is affordable, so I book a room for two nights. Tomorrow I will take another rest day and explore this interesting city. My room is paradise. It's ginormous, with a balcony and huge bathroom. By 3:30, I'm soaking in the bathtub.

After my bath, I turn my five-star hotel into a laundromat by stringing my clothes line from the shower head to the towel rack and hanging my wet clothes to dry. With a good Internet connection, I'm able to Facetime with my daughters and Gerald. It is so good to see their faces and catch up.

At dinner time, I head to the cathedral. I have no idea who I'll see, but I'm confident I'll see someone I know. I'm not disappointed. After hanging out in the cathedral for just a few minutes, I'm reunited with Dale and Becky. With them are Kris and Kate and three Germans that I haven't met yet. Together, we find a fun restaurant and enjoy a delightful meal.

In the comfort of my bed, surrounded by the room's opulence, I am pleased with the decision to take the bus. I never dreamed I would end up here, with Baly and Jose next door. I feel so supported by the Universe. Thank you Creator for this day.

Day 24

Rest Day in León

I've slept all the way to 5:30 a.m., but since I don't have to be anywhere, I roll over and sleep until 8:30. The first thing I do after waking is to step out onto the balcony to say good morning to the day. Looking around, I see I'm not alone. Jose, Mike and Andre are all doing the same thing from their perspective balconies. We laugh in unison, delighted in the magic of this shared moment.

Heading down to breakfast, I see Mike and Andre again, along with their traveling companion, Malcolm, a retired lawyer from England. The four of us enjoy the best breakfast I've eaten on the Camino yet. The buffet, included in the room rate, is served in five-star fashion. The dining room is filled with a mix of snappily dressed tourists and Pilgrims. By the questioning look on several faces at the sight of our scraggly attired group in the midst of this opulence, I can tell which tourists are unfamiliar with the Camino.

After breakfast, I return to the room for another hot bath. Hot baths and sleep have always been a cure for just about anything that ails me, and the tub is my favorite place to meditate. The hot bath doesn't help my blisters, so I use the wall to prop them above the water.

My mind is occupied by several challenges. My first is to figure out how I'm going to cover eight stages of my guidebook in seven days. When I scheduled to meet Thom and Jodi on May 15th in Sarria, I had no idea I would take two much needed rest days, along with miscalculating the time and distance it would take for me to reach Sarria. Figuring out my schedule is also imperative so that I can make advance reservations in O'Cebreiro, the village that sits on top of the mountain. Dennis has warned me that there are a limited number of places to stay, and they fill up quickly. I would hate to reach the top of the mountain and not have a bed for the night. Preferably, a comfortable one.

My second challenge is in response to Dennis' strong suggestion to lighten my load before crossing the mountain. I thought I'd crossed the highest peak in the Pyrenees, but according to Dennis and my guidebook, the upcoming mountain is a beast. Dennis has insisted, like only a good friend can, to ship as much as I can to Santiago to ease my journey over the mountain top. For the past several days, I've been practicing letting go, and I know every ounce counts. *Is there more I can release?* As a recovering control freak, I hope the hot water will soak the answers free.

After my bath, I wash more clothes and hang them on the balcony to dry. It is difficult to be inside for long after spending so many days in nature, so I plop in one of the balcony chairs, and prop my feet on the railing.

I'm hoping the fresh air and sunshine will heal the blisters on my feet and poor chapped thighs. Ever since my laundry was washed in Terradillos, my thighs have become more irritated with each day of walking. I suspect I'm having an allergic reaction to the laundry soap, and pray this day of rest will calm the inflamed skin.

I've gathered pen, guidebook, notebook and hotel stationary to continue my search for solutions to my scheduling challenge. The bath didn't provide any answers, so it's time to write morning pages. In her book, *The Artist's Way*, Julia Cameron provides directions for this powerful daily practice. Morning pages consist of writing three hand-written pages to the Creator. Her instructions are to write anything that comes to mind onto the pages. The trick is to allow unfiltered thoughts to drain from your brain. This dump is a powerful tool for unblocking creative answers, and one I haven't had time to practice on this journey.

After writing my morning pages, I make the following notes in my guidebook:

It is amazing (wondrous) how quickly the body can heal. It feels so good to just BE. My body has slowed down. I'm calmer, less frantic. So far, no earth shattering revelations, just the ability to feel more confident, more ME, in love with life, expecting the best, making choices that serve my highest good. Is it possible that my best contribution to this world is to BE the best ME that I can provide?

The morning pages' dump helps answer one question, but not the other. I still have no idea how I will navigate the eight stages in seven days, but I do know that my feet will appreciate a break by lightening my load. The past few days have been baby steps in letting go. It's time now to put my recovering control freak to the test. I scurry inside, dump my pack and scrounge the contents of my backpack for items to send to Santiago.

In just a few minutes, I separate seven items to send. The heaviest item that I don't need until Paris is the backpack cover for shipping my pack in the belly of the plane. Since I'm not planning to stay in alburgues for the remainder of the trip, I add my bedroll, towel and bedbug-proof pillowcase to the pile. The pillowcase has been totally unnecessary. I can do without a shirt, rain pants and the white cap I purchased before the trip. By removing the two heaviest and bulkiest items from my pack, I can now fit my crocs inside so they won't be swinging on the outside. Immediately, I feel better, and my excess gear hasn't even been shipped yet!

I stuff my items into the plastic hotel laundry bag and head to the front desk to ask for directions to the post office, figuring I can purchase a box there. The Parador hotel staff goes above and beyond the call of duty providing me with an empty box. I pack it with my stuff. The staff then tapes it securely closed with packing tape and gives me a map of the city, highlighting my path to the post office. Wow! I'm feeling so supported by the Universe in my decision to let go.

With my box tucked under my arm, I march through the busy streets with a big smile on my face, practically bouncing with joy. Each step is one step closer to letting go. This box is so much more than the items it holds; it represents freedom on many levels.

From Sheelagh's experience at the Pamplona post office, I know to look for a ticket as soon as I arrive. But, I'm quick to ask for help when I see an A line and a B line. Only a few people are waiting, and no one appears to be in any hurry. Neither am I. I'm enjoying this experience and don't feel the need to rush. It feels good to just BE in the moment.

I'm documenting my journey with photos, and this is a big step for me. To the amusement of the locals, when it's my turn, I ask the postmaster if I can take his picture. He looks surprised. I'm sure he doesn't get asked to have his picture taken at work very often. He poses with a shy smile and shining eyes. Following his suggestion, I send my box to the post office instead of Dennis' contact in Santiago. It is less expensive to send the box to the post office, and they hold items for thirty days without any additional cost. Since there are three post offices in Santiago, I ask the postmaster to highlight the correct location in my guidebook.

With my mission complete, I make my way back towards the cathedral to visit the tourism office located in the square. I hope to locate bus schedules and obtain information on the best way to navigate the next eight stages. But, by the time I reach the office, it's closed for siesta and the area around the cathedral is almost empty. My belly says it's time for lunch. A pasta restaurant on the main street leading from the square is open, and I'm the only customer at its outdoor café tables. Pur, my fast Swedish early-morning walking companion, asks to join me. We enjoy watching the scant Pilgrim traffic and seeing each other again. When I see the Pilgrim from Reliegos who recommended the Parador Hotel, I jump up to hug and thank him. I am so grateful for his recommendation and share its impact on my journey.

After lunch, I head back to the hotel, even though I plan to return to the square later tonight. The hotel is quite a distance from the square. Before the Camino, I would have struggled to walk the distance once. But now, with the exception of my burning chapped thighs, walking back and forth to the square is actually comforting. My body craves motion.

At the hotel, I tour the museum, discovering its magnificent, yet tragic, history. The building has served as a monastery, school, prison, horse stable, concentration camp and now a five-star hotel. Its longest use was as a stable from 1898 to 1961, housing valuable breeding studs. During its darkest history, from 1936 to 1940, during the Spanish Civil War, approximately 20,000 prisoners were held in dungeons, thousands dying inside the cold stone walls. I'm astounded to be living, even if only for two days, in a building that is older than my country.

After my tour, I return to my room to rest and actively listen for answers. Meditation turns into a nap, which recharges my mind and body. Waking up, I am unable sit still. It's time to explore León. I stop in the hallway and chat with Jose, who is leaving his room at the same time. He asks about how my rest day is going, and I share my delight in following instructions for shipping stuff to Santiago, and waiting for directions on my schedule challenge. His request, "While you are talking to God, thank Him for bringing us together," leaves me speechless and touched. My walk back to the square gives me the opportunity to fulfill Jose's request, and turn it around, thanking the Creator for so many lives who have touched mine.

It's Friday night in León. The streets are packed with families, walking arm in arm. Many are walking dogs. Every few steps, I see friends pass each other, coming from opposite directions, hug, kiss, kiss, and then off again in opposite directions, each attending to their own agenda. Street artists have lined up on several corners, performing to the delight of children, and I will admit it, the kid in me. Between the packed streets and performers, it feels like a carnival, one that I suspect that repeats every week.

Following the flow of locals, I reach the square. There aren't many Pilgrims here and I don't recognize anyone. I'm not hungry nor do I have any particular destination in mind. I continue to wander the streets, absorbing the city's energy, culture and history, feeling like an unseen ghost, witnessing life but separated from it.

Back in my room, preparing to sleep, I say my prayers. I am grateful for this Camino of Ease and Grace. I don't have to suffer; it doesn't have to be hard. I'm both nervous and excited about the upcoming days. And even though I don't have the answers, I have

Faith that they will appear, and I will recognize them when they come. God, I am ready. I am listening. I am healthy. I am loved. I am safe. I am contented. I am curious. I am enough. ALL IS WELL. Thank you for this healing day.

Email to Richard:

On my rest day I had time to ponder my trip so far. Thought you might enjoy them.

You might be a Pilgrim if...

1. You have used a bidet to soak your feet or wash your clothes.

2. You can turn a 5-star hotel into a laundromat.

3. You are willing to give and receive a piece of your heart to total strangers.

4. You look the other way when you come upon someone using emergency road facilities.

5. You respect everyone's right to walk the Camino "their" way (bus, horse, bike, motorcycle, hotel, fast, slow, healthy, hurting, blind, handicapped).

6. You are not surprised to see another Pilgrim anywhere at any time.

7. You have Faith that somehow, some way, things works out.

8. You know your body will tell you what it needs. A wise Pilgrim listens.

9. When you are caught on the trail in the rain, you know it's best to keep on walking.

10. You see that we are all travelers heading in the same direction and destination, but our paths and experiences are unique.

11. The Experience changes you.

12. You wear your pajamas to lunch and no one knows but you.

13. You try to get in bed with a French woman by mistake.

14. You know what it's like to sleep next to someone you don't know, listen to them snore all night and still be happy to see them in the future.

15. You mourn for those who don't make it.

16. You recognize less is more.

Love you,
Cindy

PART TWO

Walking in Solitude

"May the road rise up to meet you. May the wind be at your back. May the sun shine warm upon our face, and rains fall softly upon your fields. And until we meet again, may God hold you in the palm of his hands."

—**Sign from the Pilgrims' Oasis, Viana, Spain**

Day 25

Stages 21 & 22 - León to San Justo de la Vega
Total 49.4 km (30.7 miles): cab 21.8 km (13.55 miles),
walking 27.6 km (17.15 miles)

Iwake up at dark thirty, as usual. Rather than rush out the door, I will enjoy another hot bath in this paradise hotel and wait until the breakfast buffet opens to eat one more delicious meal. Truth is, I have no idea where I'm going this morning. Do I walk to the bus station or find the Camino and begin walking? I didn't receive an answer during dreamtime last night, so hopefully one more bath will provide the answer.

In the tub, I receive a download of information from the Creator. I feel like a stenographer; ideas are flooding my brain like water flowing from a fire hydrant. It's the day I've been waiting for since beginning the Camino! A children's book, business ideas, more "You might be a Pilgrim if..." ideas. Raining down so fast, the quickest way to record them is with my phone. All great ideas, but no answer on where to go from here. *Sigh.* I just have to keep trusting that somehow the answer will come, and soon.

By 7:15, I'm downstairs waiting for the restaurant door to open. The lights are off and I can't see anyone past the darkened door. At 7:30, I'm amazed when the door opens, the lights come on, and the buffet is beautifully laid out. It feels like a magic trick. Mike and his crew are back again, and we enjoy our second breakfast together.

After breakfast, I head back to the room to gather my things.

After yesterday's tour of the building, I sit for a minute, reflect on its rich history and pray the current use of providing extraordinary shelter helps erase the misery and pain endured by so many in the past. I feel like a new person and thank the space for my healing.

After checking out, I do the customary backpack swing, pat down before walking out the door with absolutely no idea of where I'm going. Sitting ten feet in front of the door is a parked cab. In all the many trips I've made in the past two days, in and out of the building, this is the first time I've seen a car parked here, much less a cab.

I recognize it as the sign I've been waiting for and immediately turn around to find the bellman to inquire if I can hire the cab to take me to Villar de Mazarife, which is 21.8 km away. My guidebook shows that if I cab to the end of stage 21, walk the 31.2 km to Astorga tonight, I'm on target to meet Thom and Jodi. It will be a long day, but doable.

Unfortunately, the cab is not available. The bellman assures me he can have another one here in three minutes. Without hesitation, I make the request and am amazed that a cab shows up in no time. Thirty minutes later, I'm in Villar de Mazarife, ready to begin the second half of my day. It is so humbling to know that an entire day's effort is just a thirty minute cab ride.

I'm excited about walking this portion of the Camino. I'm looking forward to crossing the medieval bridge in Puente de Órbigo. I'm also a bit concerned about spending the night in Astorga. An American woman is missing and was last seen leaving Astorga on April 5th. No one knows where she is or what happened to her. I'm praying for her safe return soon. Despite her disappearance, I'm unconcerned about my safety, but my intuition is telling me to be alert in Astorga. I'm uncomfortable about the city itself.

I'm conscious of how quickly things change. It feels weird to be going so fast in the cab. The ride is short, but the change is profound. After being semi-stationary in a busy, vibrant city, I've been delivered in a fast cab ride, and now I'm back walking in the stillness of the countryside. The dramatic change of pace is a head spinner. Those who spent the night here last night left long ago. I'm back to being off cycle with other walkers, again. I'm alone and loving it.

The farther I walk, the more removed I feel from the fast pace of León. In the first hour, I'm passed by five cars, three dump trucks, one tour bus and two tractors. I can't say it's quieter yet, but it is a slower pace.

Today is frog day, LOUD frog day. The irrigation ditches running parallel to the road on both sides are filled with male frogs looking for a date, proclaiming their presence in stereo. I wonder what the frog symbolizes and will text Kim my animal spirit wrangler, later for the answer.

In Cruce, a cross street divides the Camino from pavement to gravel road and slows the pace even more. The irrigation ditches are gone, as well as the accompanying racket of croaks. The traffic slows even more. I'm passed by one car, two bicycle Pilgrims, and one motorcycle before reaching Villavante.

Entering Villavante, I feel at home at the sight of four whimsical whirligigs. They remind me of my own, mounted on top of a cedar fence next to the pool, twirling in the wind. These whirligigs are mounted on the red tile roof of a brown, mud-colored building with an elderly gentleman sitting in the shade of the porch. He is the only person visible on the street. He silently watches me as I pass without acknowledging my existence.

This sleepy agriculture village offers few opportunities to stop for a much needed break. A sign that says "Bar" with empty red chairs out front looks like my best shot to use indoor plumbing. It's my last chance for another 4.5 km. The bar is empty when I enter, and I call "Buen Camino!" in hopes that someone will come out. Normally in a bar like this, there would be croissants or other food items for sale, but here there are none. When the proprietress appears, I order a beer and water to justify my use of the bathroom. The toilet lacks a seat, but it's inside, so I'm happy.

After changing socks, working my feet and making a second trip to the bathroom to get rid of the beer, I continue my journey. When I enter the next town, Hospital de Órbigo, I'm excited to see the medieval bridge. It looks just like the picture in my guidebook, except better because I'm actually on the bridge, walking across centuries of history. Creating my history.

The bridge is one of the longest and best preserved medieval bridges, built on top of a Roman bridge, crossing over the Rio Órbigo. The bridge has a rich history of battles, scorned love and lost honor. According to my guidebook, a legendary knight, Don Suero de Quiñones, broke 300 lances in one month to defend his honor when his lady dumped him. What I don't understand is why did the opposing knights show up to fight? The bridge has also been attributed to inspiring the story of Don Quixote.

Hospital de Órbigo is a village of 1100 people, and according to my map, it is halfway to Astorga, and the best place to get lunch. It's going to be a long day, and I need more fuel than beer and water if I'm going to make it. By following my instincts, I locate a café off the Camino route that looks promising. For the second time today, I am the only person in the restaurant. While waiting for my meal, I call several promising hotels in Astorga to book a room. One hotel answers, puts me on hold, and after waiting for several minutes, I hang up in frustration. I have limited minutes on my phone plan and don't want to waste them on hold. The other hotel doesn't answer. Is this a sign? The Pilgrim meal is delicious, and despite the lovely furnishings of the room, I remove my shoes to roll the pain from the bottom of my feet. The good news is there is no one to offend by taking my shoes off.

I have a choice in paths to reach Astorga: one that follows the N-120, or I can take a natural path. After the busyness of the past two days, my soul longs for the solitude of the natural path. Today is the last stage of the Meseta, and here, standing on the first rise above it, I'm amazed at how good it feels to be past it. I can't believe it, but I'm actually looking forward to the mountains ahead. The Meseta was easier walking and beautiful, but there is something to be said for elevation and the inspiration that comes from a hilltop view.

The pace slows again. With the exception of occasional bike riders, who look surprised to see me as they whiz past, I have the Camino to myself, and the Creator who made this glorious natural beauty. Purple and yellow flowers are in bloom, and despite my long distance to cover today, I stop to capture their beauty. The afternoon sun has warmed up the day, creating a river of sweat, which isn't a problem until I reach the first valley.

The valley cuts off the breeze and I'm instantly attacked by swarming mosquitoes. I'm not carrying bug spray and haven't needed any until now. I'm surrounded by a moving black cloud. Mosquitoes fly so close to my face, I'm afraid I'll swallow them. To prevent this, I blow air, like blowing out a candle, with each exhale, hoping to create a bug-free air space to inhale. My only protection is to outwalk them and continue blowing out each breath. At the top of the valley, the breeze blows the mosquitoes away and I slow down to a normal pace. I face three more mosquito-filled valleys before reaching Astorga.

In places, the natural path is difficult to determine because of road construction. There are no yellow arrows to be found. Yikes! Instead, rocks have been painted yellow and placed on top of mounded dirt caused by the road construction. Fearful that I'm lost, I backtrack several times to find the last yellow rock and keep my eyes peeled for additional rocks. In the midst of green fields and flowers, the Camino leads straight through a veal farm. A sight that saddens me greatly. Seeing baby calves, isolated from their mothers, penned up side by side under the shade of an igloo dog house, is heart breaking. I don't plan to eat veal ever again.

At Cruceiro Santo Toribio, the highest point of today's stage, I stop to take a picture of the cross that stands tall against the cloudy sky. The valley below is filled with civilization. I'm close to my destination. This is great news, because I'm exhausted. It's been a long day of mixed emotions. Excitement to see the bridge, fighting bugs, seeing the reality of veal production and being alone with the Creator.

San Justo is less than 4 km from Astorga, but before I complete the journey, I make another attempt to reserve a room. I'm uncomfortable to continue without a reservation. Neither hotel I call will answer the phone. My intuition tells me to spend the night here, specifically at the single-star hotel called Hostal Julia. Dragging my tired body across the street, I inquire about a room.

I am warmly greeted by the owner and follow her up two flights of stairs to a room that feels more like a dungeon. To be fair, after my room at the Parador, just about any room would not compare favorably. The room is just wide enough for the saggy, full-sized bed and single bedside table. Curtain sheers mute the natural sunlight trying to come into the room, and the stained plastic shower floor makes me shudder, wishing I still had my shower shoes. On the bedside table is a glass ashtray. The kind I last saw in the 1970s when both my parents smoked. Feeling dubious about my room, I check in with the Creator again and receive the same answer. I am where I'm supposed to be. I am asked to have Faith, to trust without knowing why.

Heading downstairs, I see a Pilgrim couple, who I've never seen before, waiting for dinner. I head to the bar, order a beer and watch the meal preparation for the other couple. I am grateful for the nice lunch today, because after watching the cook, I know this beer, and one more to fill me up, is the safest dinner I can order tonight.

The TV in the bar area is blaring, disturbing my eardrums. I prefer the privacy of my room to write my daily notes, but couldn't find a working plug to recharge my phone, so I'm charging it in the bar. It reeks of cigarette smoke, and I wonder, what is my lesson tonight?

Unable to take the noise for long, I retreat to my room. As I enter, I notice the TV on the wall and realize I can unplug it to charge my phone. Before climbing into bed, following instructions from my intuition, I pull the covers down and spray the sheets with Thieves spray. My sense is there may be bedbugs. Thieves© from Young Living Essential Oils is an ancient formula of essential oils that protected looters during the plague. I've been carrying it all this time, and tonight is the first time I've felt the need to use it. It has been a long day of bridges, bugs and beer, and I wonder again, *Why am I here? What is my lesson tonight?*

Day 26

Stages 22 & 23 - San Justo de la Vega to Rabanal del Camino 24.2 km (15.03 miles)

I'm out the door by 7:00 and curious to learn why I was directed to stay at Hostal Julia last night. By the time I reach Astorga, I have my answer. It's only 3.6 km away, but by the time I arrive, I can see that this last stretch was beyond my capabilities last night. The Camino is teaching me to trust my intuition. Seeing the answer in the early dawn of light is a gift. Receiving these instant answers makes it easier to trust. Something to remember when I get home.

Spain's commitment to the modern day Pilgrim is amazing, ingenious and appreciated. A giant green elevated ramp, reminding me of a Lego toy from a distance, has been built to safely move Pilgrims over the railroad tracks.

Three ramps on each side provide the necessary height to clear the tracks. I stop at the top, stand over the tracks and imagine how exciting it would be to be here with a train rumbling under my feet.

My Spidey senses are on alert today. Intuition is instructing me to stay in sight of other Pilgrims on this part of the Camino, which is ironic after yesterday's ease in total solitude through the barren countryside. I'm not afraid. I'm smart and listen by adjusting my pace to stay in sight of other Pilgrims.

After a delicious chocolate croissant and orange juice to make up for last night's missed meal, I follow the train of Pilgrims through the deserted Sunday morning streets of Astorga. On the other side of city, entering the countryside, I keep my eyes peeled for signs of the missing Pilgrim girl and send prayers for her safe return.

I stop in Murias de Rechivaldo for a more filling breakfast. I'm enchanted by the woman behind the counter. I have no idea if she is the owner or an employee, but she has the face of an angel and passion for creating healthy shakes and delicious food for her guests.

While waiting for my meal, I review my guidebook to see if I can make a reservation for tonight. The first "other" accommodation listed in the book is a casa rural, and with one phone call, I have a private room booked. What a difference a day makes. I'm relieved to know I have a bed to myself tonight.

Next, I connect to Wi-Fi, post an update and check on my family on Facebook. Today is Mother's Day. My daughter, Tiffany, calculating the time difference, posted a Mother's Day greeting to me last night. The next post I see is from the National Speakers Association North Texas (NSA-NT). The monthly meeting was yesterday and they posted encouraging pictures of posters they made for me. Seeing the two posts, back to back, bring me to tears. *Why do I cry when people show they love and care for me?*

At breakfast, the serving of tortilla is extra large and served with bread and fruit. I can't eat it all. The Spanish Tortilla has become my favorite food. It is nothing like Texas tortillas; it's more like a potato pie. Had I known, I would have skipped the croissant in Astorga. I bus my own table on the way to the bathroom and am surprised on my way out when Angel Face stops me and hands me my leftovers neatly wrapped in paper. I thank her for the food and her angelic presence.

In Santa Catalina de Somoza, I stop for a sock change and a beer. I can't remember when or where this habit of beer stops started, but they must be working since I'm able to crank out 30-km days with Ease and Grace. The table of Spanish speaking Pilgrims next to me is enjoying a carafe of wine, so I'm not drinking alone at 10:45 in the morning. Not that I need to justify drinking a beer after walking 12 km. I feel like I've earned it.

The noise from the table next to me escalates. The people around the table are having fun and enjoying each other's company. At first, I can't understand a word they're saying. Then the subject matter changes. A conversation about farts needs no interpretation. My laughter catches the attention of the speaker, who turns to me, smiles and switches to English to include me in the additional hilarious details to his story. God, I love the Camino community. The humor, the shared experiences, the similarities between people and generosity of spirit.

On the other side of the village, an artisan has set up shop on the trail. Seated at a table, he hand-carves clay shells and crosses to string onto cords for necklaces. In the past, I walked right past similar vendors, but not today. Wearing a brown apron, the artisan has graying hair, a stubby beard and kind eyes behind round glasses. It's his essence of a Spanish craftsman that stops me. Dennis gave me a packet of seeds a few days ago as a gift. A shell from this artist, crafted here on the Camino, would make a perfect gift for Dennis, so I make my donation and pick out the shell that I think Dennis will enjoy.

My animal companions today include the crow, cuckoo and lizard. According to the pages that Kim sent, each spirit animal has multiple meanings. They all seem accurate, but for the crow I have narrowed it down to three meanings. According to the book, when the crow shows up I am on the verge of manifesting something I've been working on for a while, or I need to expect a big change, or get a glimpse into some future event that directly affects me. Either way, when crow shows up, I feel lucky.

The cuckoo's meaning to me for this trip is crystal clear. The cuckoo is reminding me that I don't have to suffer to grow and mature in my spiritual path. Each *cuckoo, cuckoo* is encouraging me to enjoy my journey with Ease and Grace!

Like the crow, the lizard's meaning is multi-faceted. When lizard shows up, I am to listen to my own intuition over anyone else's, or I am to meditate on my most ancient part and ask to be shown a vision of my life path. Or to be aware of the sights, sounds and vibrations around me and be selective of who I allow into my space. Bottom line, when the lizard shows up, I realize I'm supposed to pay attention. While the exact meanings may be muddy, I appreciate their company and enjoy each *caw, cuckoo, cuckoo* and rustling in the bushes.

In El Ganso, I'm tempted to stop at the brightly decorated Cowboy Bar. It looks inviting. The rest of the village is full of crumbling homes, whose walls and doors remain intact despite their missing roofs. I'm more than a little curious about the bar, even though I'm not hungry, thirsty or in need of indoor plumbing. Rather than satisfy my curiosity, I keep moving forward, focused on reaching my destination. Yesterday, I fell short on making my goal to the stage end, so today I'm committed to making it to Rabanal del Camino. I feel confident in my ability to do so, as long as I stay focused on forward motion.

At Puente de Pañote, the smooth path turns into a rocky trail littered with twisted roots protruding from the ground. I'm battling fatigue but fight through it, knowing I'm on the homestretch for the day. The wire fence next to the trail has been decorated with crosses made from fallen sticks, some decorated with bits of colorful material. It's like walking through an art gallery, dedicated to the Creator. I can't help but enjoy their inspirational beauty as I pass.

From experience, I know that I should walk or take in the scenery, but not do both. I'm pushing myself to keep the Pilgrim couple ahead of me in sight, which isn't easy because they're faster than me. My Spidey senses to keep other Pilgrims in sight have calmed down, but still, I prefer to keep up with them, if I can.

And then it happens. My left foot catches on the tip of a tree root and unleashes a top-heavy forward motion fall that cannot be stopped. My walking sticks are unable to leverage against the unexpected force and collapse to each side. My backpack feels like a giant hand is pushing me down to the ground. In slow motion. My brain understands what is about to happen before it happens, and knows the fall can't be stopped. On my way down, I involuntarily scream, "OHHHHHH SHHHHIIIITTTTT!!"

I face-plant on the trail. My eye glasses shatter into pieces. I roll over on my back, sit up and hope the only things broken are my glasses. The young couple ahead must have heard me cry out, because they've run back to see if I need any help. I tell them I'm OK, but accept the young man's assistance in getting up. They look concerned, but I assure them I'll be fine. Now, I just have to convince myself.

My face hurts. I feel a trickle of blood. Using the selfie mode of my camera, I see that I have a minor cut near my left eye and another on my cheek. I can feel a bruise already forming. After taking a tentative step to make sure everything else is in working order, I'm relieved that I'm not in too much pain.

My glasses are in two pieces, the plastic wire supporting my left lens has broken, so I stuff them in the cloth glass holder in my belly pack. Gathering my scattered items, hat, walking sticks and dignity, I slowly limp up the trail, feeling lucky. It could've been so much worse. I say a prayer of gratitude to Grace for protecting me during my fall. This will be a Mother's Day I won't forget. I've been given the lesson: "Multi-tasking does not pay." It becomes my mantra for the rest of the day.

By the time I reach the casa rural at 2:15, I feel cooked. The hospitalero can see my pain, offers to show me to my room immediately and says I can pay after I'm rested. I follow him slowly up the stairs and collapse on the bed after he leaves. I don't rest long, anxious to see what I've done to my body. I strip and take a hot shower. I'm pleased to discover that my only injuries are limited to bruises on my left leg and hip.

After my shower, I dress in my pajamas and gingerly descend the steep stairs to pay for my room and inquire about a clothes line to hang my clothes on. The hospitalero tells me he will put one out front. My khaki pants have pink skid marks on the left hip from my fall. I definitely won't buy brightly colored underwear again that continues to bleed color. Sheesh.

I tiptoe back up the stairs, wash my clothes and schlep down again to hang my laundry on the clothes line. It's a bit humiliating to hang my hot pink granny panties on Main Street.

While my clothes are drying, I retreat to my room. It's time to see what I can do about my glasses. I remove the pieces from their holder, run them under hot water in the sink and dry them. I can't see well enough without my glasses to fix them properly, so I do the best I can by touch and feel. Using white medical tape, I tape the lens back to the frames and test its sturdiness. While it's not great, and I won't be able to walk in them, it's steady enough to use to read my guidebook for directions.

Now that I know I'm OK and have fixed my glasses, it's time to tell Gerald that I face-planted on the Camino. I take a selfie with my taped up glasses, and text the picture to Gerald with the message, "Notice anything new?"

His response cracks me up. "Did you get a haircut?"

"Look again," I text.

"Are your glasses crooked?"

After my conversation with Gerald, I check on my clothes and head down the street to a bar for an early Pilgrim meal. My casa rural offers dinner tonight at 7:00 p.m., but I plan to go to bed early. I'm beat, literally. The meal is delicious and I feel better afterwards.

Sitting on a bench, across from the casa rural, in my newly taped-up glasses, I pour over my guidebook to calculate distances. Then, using my minimal Spanish, I make reservations for the final week of my journey with Thom and Jodi. I surprise myself that I'm successful in making several reservations. I feel I've stretched myself beyond what I thought I was capable of. Again, I'm amazed at the growth I'm experiencing on the Camino that has nothing to do with walking.

After gathering my dry clothes from the line, brushing my teeth and taking a preventative Tylenol with Codeine, I make my final preparations for tomorrow. It will be a big day, one I've spent months preparing for. Tomorrow is Cruce de Ferro Day, the day I will leave behind the rock I've been carrying from home. What will I leave behind with the rock? Writing an email to Richard helps.

Richard,

I made it to Rabanal today. Tomorrow I climb the highest peak on the trip to leave a rock that I've carried with me from home. I brought a Texas Heart rock that Gerald found on the property. Leaving the rock is symbolic of leaving any problem or issue that you would like to release. I plan to leave behind beliefs that do not serve me, like limiting beliefs and blocks that keep me from my highest good. And

I want to leave behind judgments about others and myself. Forgive myself for past decisions. Decisions that were the best I could do at the time, but decisions that I've regretted.

Thanks for being a listening ear. This has helped me clarify my thoughts.

I'm more than 2/3 done!!

Love you.
Cindy

Life can change in an instant. What started as a great day remained a great day. After falling and breaking my glasses, I have more appreciation of how fragile life is. Dear Creator, thank you for the ability to continue.

Day 27

Stage 24 - Rabanal del Camino to Molinaseca
26.2 km (16.3 miles)

In dreamtime, I received the following prayer for my rock. After waking up, I capture it on paper.

I am leaving behind feelings, thoughts, beliefs, habits and releasing emotional baggage that blocks or limits my Highest Self. Thank you. Cynthia D. Arledge. I forgive myself and others.

Today is expected to be warmer than usual and I have more than 25 km to walk. There are two uphill climbs and a significantly steep downhill section. Dennis warned me about this section. He is planning to take the road and has encouraged me to do the same. I haven't made up my mind yet. I'll wait to see how I feel. The Tylenol must have helped, because surprisingly I'm not too sore.

By 7:15, the sun is rising, and I've already put thirty minutes of walking on the day. I'm super stoked about getting such an early start, until I realize that I've left my hat hanging on the hook on the back of my door. In my haste to beat the heat, I skipped my normal pat down. It's decision time. Do I go back for the hat or just keep going? I had another hat but shipped it to Santiago. Oops. Looking at the map, it's doubtful that I'll be able buy a new one until day's end.

The hat is already sad looking, so I don't mind leaving it. The pins I purchased as souvenirs would be great to have, but I'm not sure they're worth an hour of walking back and forth to retrieve them. But then, I remember the angel pin that belonged to Dad. That pin is worth the effort.

While walking back on the Camino, going against the grain of my fellow Pilgrims, I receive questioning looks. "Forgot my hat" brings nods of understanding and looks of empathy for the duplicate effort. At the casa rural, I'm happy to find my hat exactly where I left it. Removing it from the hook, I take a moment to gaze at the angel pin and connect with my parents. The top of my hat is caked in dried dirt. As I brush the dust away, I quickly realize I could have easily lost the pin during yesterday's face-plant. Man, I would've been UPSET if I'd walked all the way back here to get the pin, only to find that I'd lost it yesterday. Whew, dodged that bullet.

My second trip up the trail is less enjoyable than the first. Even though I consciously made the decision to return for the angel pin, the effort of retracing my steps up the steep hill has unleashed a monster. The idea that I "lost time" and could be farther down the road grows with each step, robbing me of my tranquility and happiness. Unable to take the internal chatter anymore, I stop, mentally and physically shake myself and reclaim my power, my peace.

"Nothing is lost. All is well. I am exactly where I'm supposed to be. Breathe."

It's a matter of choice, a change in attitude. I make the decision to be happy, and let go of the belief that I've lost time. Doing so allows me the freedom to enjoy the incredible purple flowers in bloom, the views from the ridges and enjoyment of the moment. I am so fortunate that I can walk after yesterday's fall, and now I feel fortunate to have escaped the mind trap that was dragging me down.

It's 9:00 a.m. by the time I reach Foncebadón, and I'm ready to stop for a bite at the first café I see. Inside, there's not much food left, and I am grateful to order one of the last delicious looking muffins to enjoy on the outdoor patio. I'm surrounded by Pilgrims I've never seen before. It feels strange after traveling for so long with the same group.

On my way out of town, I see the young couple who picked me up from the trail yesterday. They are happy to know I wasn't injured and allow me to take a picture of them. My collection of Camino Angels is growing. The path out of Foncebadón leads up and over a majestic countryside of beautiful flower-filled fields, breathtaking views, each more beautiful than the next. My Spidey senses are quiet, and in spite of yesterday's fall, I'm comfortable walking alone.

Cruz de Ferro is nothing like I imagined, and nothing like the scene from *The Way*. In the movie, the group of Pilgrims walking together had an emotional moment, almost a ceremony, to leave their rocks/burdens behind in fierce weather conditions.

My reality feels more like Disneyland on the Camino. It's a beautiful sunshiny day. A loud group of Pilgrims surrounds the cross. I can hear laughter and shouts. People are scrambling up the pile to have their picture taken. I debate whether to wait until the crowd dissipates to take my turn or just leave my rock and move on. Seeing another group of Pilgrims coming up the trail nudges me towards leaving my rock. I hurry up the pile, say the dreamtime prayer, breathe and add my rock, in its blue sack, to the top of pile. After taking a quick photo of the rock and my surroundings, I escape to the comfort and solitude of the trail. Even though it wasn't what I expected, I do feel significantly lighter.

At the highest point of today's hike, the rocky path climbs to join a paved road. An enterprising entrepreneur has transformed a camper trailer into a mobile café. The plastic tables and chairs out front are full. Additional Pilgrims stand outside the trailer, patiently waiting their turn to order or fill a seat as it empties.

In the grass next to the cafe, an unattended but saddled donkey enjoys unlimited access to the succulent green grass. A tri-colored Jack Russell Terrier sits atop soft folded blankets, alert to her surroundings, as if guarding her much larger companion. I suspect there's a costumed human to accompany the animals, but cannot locate him or her in the crowd.

After my recent Disneyland/Cruz de Ferro experience, I have no desire to join the crowd. I keep on walking. The rocky path begins its descent, flowers crowding the path. I gingerly pick my way through the shifting loose rocks, learning how to walk without glasses. I can see the big stuff, like trees; I just can't see the small stuff, like leaves and gravel that want to slip out from under my feet.

Since passing the mobile café, I've been traveling with a new companion, Zoe from Virginia. She is on holiday from Paris where she teaches English. I'm thrilled to spend time with her and hear her story. It feels like we're on top of the world, just the two us. We take turns taking each other's pictures on this amazing stretch of Earth.

I'm confused to hear the whine of multiple weed trimmers echoing from below the ridge. Cresting the rise, I see a crew of men, wearing yellow safety vests, red hard hats and bandanas, wrestling giant trimmers, creating a cyclone of flowers and leaves, exposing a wider path for Pilgrims to enjoy. Another example of the dedication of resources to support Pilgrims and their journey.

In Acebo, I say goodbye to my new friend. Zoe sees friends she knows at the first café. Rather than tag along, I continue on to the next café where I spot the delightful French couple. We reunite with the usual hug and cheek kiss. We sit together and enjoy a round of cold beers, smiling at each other.

Leaving Acebo, the Camino follows the road long enough for me to know I'm not taking Dennis' advice to walk the road to Molinaseca. My eyes have adjusted to walking without glasses, and I'm not sore from my fall yesterday. The cuckoo and lizard are keeping me company. When the natural path veers to the left, I don't hesitate to follow the yellow arrows leading across the open fields of flowers.

The village of Riego de Ambrós is deserted. Man, they take siesta seriously here. The only other Pilgrim I see is a California girl named Neinel. I saw her last night in Rabanal while eating dinner but didn't get a chance to meet her. We introduce ourselves and decide to walk to Molinaseca together. The trail is so dangerous here, now I understand why Dennis urged me to take the road. This is, without a doubt, the toughest section of the Camino yet. The rocks are huge, some jutting out of the ground, higher than our heads. It feels like I'm walking on the bones of the Earth. And it's the most fun I've had yet!

We stagger into Molinaseca at 3:45. I'm exhausted and

exhilarated at the same time. As we enter town, I see people playing in the river. It looks like a perfect ending to the day and a part of me wishes I had more energy and time to join them. On the bridge, I say goodbye to Neinel. She is young and plans to walk on. Our walk together was short but impactful. We spent the majority of our time talking and watching out for each other on the tough section of the trail. Another name to add to my Camino Angel list.

I have a private room reserved at the same hotel that Dennis is staying in, and I plan to meet him for dinner tonight. My room is on the top floor. It's huge, with three twin beds and a skylight. The bathroom is even better. Its white tile walls reflect light through another skylight. It's not the river, but it does have a huge bathtub and a bidet to soak my feet in cold water. Ahhhh.

Before meeting Dennis for dinner, I remove the white medial tape from my glasses and replace it with pink sports tape. My broken lens keeps falling out. I hope the sports tape works better so that I don't lose the lens. And the pink tape really makes a fashion statement.

Dennis helps me restock my cash by leading me to the ATM. He has helped me in so many ways, I can't imagine what this trip would have been like without him. We've been walking together, on and off, for over 500 km now. We are getting so close to our destination, and yet the "official" Camino, the last 100 km, has not even begun.

Our dinner conversation includes making plans to stay in touch for the next ten days. I hope that we'll see each other in Santiago. We will walk 22 km together tomorrow to Cacabelos, where Dennis will spend the night. I will walk an additional 10 km to Villafranca del Bierzo, so I can stay on target to meet Thom and Jodi. I give Dennis the shell necklace that I purchased and tell him the story of how it survived the fall on Mother's Day.

We laugh, a lot. He shares about his terrific time in Foncebadón last night, and I keep him laughing with my adventures. And pink glasses. After dinner, we make plans to meet at 6:45 in the morning.

Back in my room, I think about how far I've come and the remaining journey. It seems like I've walked more than one Camino. The first Camino ended three days ago in León. Today is Day Three of my second Camino. And I instinctively know I will walk a third Camino when Thom and Jodi join me.

Day 28

Stage 25 - Molinaseca to Villafranca del Bierzo
30.6 km (19.01 miles)

There was no need to set an alarm last night. Church bells woke me up, every hour on the hour. The hotel is next to the church, and the bell tower looms right above my room. Earplugs can't compete with the *clang-clang-clang* reverberating through my skylight. I get up and am packed and ready to meet Dennis at 6:45. We step into the predawn light with anticipation for another fantastic day on the Camino and our last to walk together.

Molinaseca is basically a suburb of Ponferrada, so the day begins with concrete walking. Dennis takes the lead today, and I'm happy to discover that I can physically keep up with him now. As long as I don't stop and take too many pictures. He teases me about the quality and quantity of my photographs. None of them will win any awards, but that is not their purpose. Their purpose is to bring me back to a particular moment in time. I even took a picture of the tree root that I tripped on and the crosses I was looking at when I fell. Although it's not a moment I'm liable to forget, the image of the crosses takes me to the joy I felt seeing them—right before the fall. They also remind me multitasking does not pay.

As we draw closer to Ponferrada, a city of 69,000, Dennis has chosen the natural path that circles around the city, instead of the shorter, direct, all-concrete route that cuts through the city center.

This path sits higher than the city, so as we circle around, enjoying a rotating view, we never get any closer. It's hard to tell if we're making any progress. After what feels like forever, we make a final turn that leads into the city, past a castle. A *real* fortress that actually looks like a castle, making me wish I had time to explore its interior. After almost two hours, we reach the main plaza and stop for breakfast.

Our choice for breakfast is limited to chocolate croissant or plain croissant. The bar looks like it caters to the night crowd and just happens to be open during breakfast. We are the only two patrons, and quickly agree this is a good stop for indoor plumbing, a juice and a croissant. It's just enough fuel to keep us going. We'll eat a second breakfast farther down the road.

We walk another 9 km and enter Camponaraya. Dennis remembers a café he enjoyed last year and knows how to get there. He reminds me of Gerald. They both have this ability to return to a place they have only been to once. The café is filled with patrons, mainly Pilgrims, but a few locals as well. We settle in for a delicious hot breakfast, sock change and chat. If all goes according to plan, in 5 km we will say "Buen Camino," and not see each other again for nine days.

Last night at dinner, Dennis was happy to hear I had followed his advice and shipped a package to Santiago. While waiting for our breakfast, he picks up my pack to check its weight, and looks like a proud papa. My plan is to reach O'Cebreiro tomorrow. The final 8 km looks brutal, especially on the heels of a 20-km hike. Although I'm happy that my pack is lighter, I'm hoping that I don't have to carry it on this section. As an experienced horsewoman, I hope to cover this portion of the Camino by horseback and let my horse do the heavy lifting.

I first learned about riding horses on the Camino in Sonia Croquette's book, *Walking Home*. In the past few days on Facebook, my friends Adam and Pete, the Australians I met in Larrasoaña, have both posted about their separate, but wonderful, horse experiences. My intention is to enjoy this steepest portion of the Camino, with Ease and Grace, astride a beloved equine.

After breakfast, the path finally turns to natural path. Today's concrete walking has been no fun and has killed my feet. I would gladly repeat yesterday's dangerous and downward rocky trail over this concrete jungle. For the first time on this journey, I'm wondering, *Why did I do this?* The people I interviewed before my trip said this moment would come. What is it about today, besides the concrete, that has me questioning myself?

We reach Cacabelos by 1:30, and while Dennis gets settled in his hotel, I sip a cold beer in the restaurant and work the kinks out of my feet. I look for friends in the steady stream of Pilgrims passing under my window. Across the street, I see Tanja sitting in a chair, engrossed with her phone. Knowing she can't see me through the dark glass, I snap her picture. If I had my shoes on, or if my feet didn't hurt so badly, I'd make the effort to cross the street to say "hi" and receive the big hug that I know she has for me. Instead, I'm confident I'll see her again and remind myself to relax. I still have another 10 km to go today, and I need this time to rest, rejuvenate and contemplate today's question.

When Dennis arrives, we enjoy a last beer together before I head out for the final leg of today's journey. In the short time we have together, we make final plans to email each other and stay in touch until we hopefully see each other again in Santiago.

The question is still gnawing on my soul. I still have another 10 km to go after leaving Dennis. I feel confident I can make it, but am still wondering, *Why AM I doing this?* In Pieros, I have to make a choice. Do I take the shorter road route or the longer natural path? Robert Frost's poem "The Road Not Taken" comes to mind, and as if following his directions, I turn right onto the natural path. It does, indeed, make all the difference.

It feels so redundant to keep thinking that I'm walking through the most beautiful countryside I've ever seen, but I can't help it. The variety of beauty is apparently unending. Yesterday's wild mosaic of color has been replaced with row after row of grapevines. The red dirt contrasts sharply between the straight lines of sprouting green leaves, promising a fall harvest of fruit. This valley of cultivated fields is surrounded by a ring of purple mountains—purple from the flowers in full bloom that I walked through yesterday.

It is in the contrast of landscapes that I discover the answer to my question of why I'm here. It's hope for a harvest. Not just for the Camino, but life in general. The difference in the landscape was created by hard work and determination in the hope and expectation of receiving a harvest. A positive result of consistent efforts to produce the fruit of their labor. My journey is about hard work and determination in the hope and expectation of cultivating my soul. The fruit of my labor is the fulfillment of my dreams, achieved by the effort that I'm willing to put into them.

As the path begins to climb, cultivated fields end abruptly with clear demarcation lines separating them from the native vegetation and trees. It's hot today and I'm confused by a pile of white that has accumulated among the green underbrush at the base of the trees ahead. It looks like a bank of snow. Entering the forest, I recognize the snow is actually Cottonwood seeds. I have never seen this much of it come down at one time. I stop to enjoy the experience of allowing the delicate fluff to kiss my face as it drifts by.

Finding the answer to my *why* reenergizes me, but my energy doesn't last long. Now that I have the answer that plagued me all day, the reality of the long walk is kicking in, and the long climb into town drains me. As I pass an alburgue on my right, I notice a woman wearing a pair of shorts lying in waist-high grass with an arm over her face, underneath the clothes line. She looks like I feel, exhausted, but no matter how exhausted I get, I can't imagine lying in grass, in shorts. I feel itchy just seeing her do it.

The cobblestone streets are beautiful to look at but horrible on the feet, especially after walking 30 km. It feels like I'm tiptoeing on glass shards. Thin flat stones have been laid down the middle of the road. I try to walk on them instead of the cobblestones, but it's not a satisfactory method because I have to walk heel to toe to stay in the middle. Besides looking goofy, it's harder to walk this way than walking on the cobblestone.

By the time I reach my hotel, it's 4:30 and I'm exhausted. My room has two full beds pushed together. The decor is a delightful mix of old and new. I've been communicating with several friends using WhatsApp and am delighted to discover Dale and Becky are in town. I have time to do laundry, shower and shop for food for tomorrow's journey before meeting them for dinner.

We enjoy heart-to-heart conversations filled with laughter and joy. I respect them so much and am Blessed by their company. We make plans to eat dinner tomorrow night in O'Cebreiro and head to our respective night's lodgings, well into the darkness. Tomorrow is a big day but I'm feeling up to the challenge. I seem to be running on water, beer and bread. Thank you, Creator, for your support and co-creation of love.

Email to Richard:

I walked 30.6 km over some hills today and still feel good! I must be getting stronger.

I re-taped my glasses and hope they last until I get home and can buy some new ones. It was on my list to do since these are 5 years old, or more.

Glad to hear you are moving forward with your motion, and that you're OK with support from family.

I love you,
Cindy

Day 29

Stage 26 - Villafranca del Bierzo to O'Cebreiro
Total 30.1 km (18.7 miles): walking, 21.9 km (13.6 miles),
horse, 8.2 km (5.1 miles)

It's going to be a doozy of a day. But centered in my *why* and refreshed from a few hours of sleep, I feel up to today's challenge, especially if I'm able to manifest a horse for the steepest and final 8 km of the trail. The hill must be challenging, because for the first time, I have to reconfirm my reservations by 2:00 and guarantee my arrival to keep my reservation. That tells me that more often than not, Pilgrims anticipate making it to the top and fail.

Leaving the hotel, I return to the square where I met Dale and Becky last night, and follow a narrow alleyway that will lead me to the Camino. Between my crooked eyeglasses, the dark, narrow alleyways, tall rock buildings blocking the view, and the up and down of hills, along with my rush to get on with the day, I'm lost. And I'm not alone. A trio has joined me in my hunt for the route. Truth is they're really looking for coffee, and their best opportunity to find a café open this early is to find the Camino trail. It becomes a treasure hunt in the dark, searching for hidden markers. After walking all the way around the square, at last one of the Pilgrims finds an arrow that leads us to the Camino. I had passed that marker earlier and failed to notice it. After 29 days on the Camino, I can't believe that I'm having this much trouble finding the route. I am humbled, again.

Coming around the corner, I see a side view of the bridge

crossing the Rio Burbia. Street lights on the bridge shine merrily and lead to a single lit building. All the other buildings surrounding it remain stubbornly dark, refusing to join in this early dawn celebration of another day. Mountains ring the city, blocking the view of the rising sun. I imagine today will look like God gradually turning up the dimmer switch of daylight.

The river is lined with multi-story, balconied buildings crowding its banks on both sides. It has the look and feel of a resort town, with the river at the center of attention. Stopping to enjoy the view, I imagine what it would be like to sit on one of the balconies. I can picture myself, coffee cup in hand, listening to the sound of rushing water and watching the stream of Pilgrims crossing this bridge and wondering about their story. Who are they? What is their journey about? But, that is a dream, and today I am the Pilgrim crossing the bridge with miles to go and an important decision to make on the other side of the bridge.

The guidebook shows I have three routes leaving Villafranca. The first route is a remote, long, all-natural path that drops into Herrerías. Pete posted about this on Facebook several days ago. It looks amazing, but I'm not up to the level of fitness that this route demands, so I eliminate this option. The second route is road walking on the flat valley floor. The flatness is enticing, and I know it will make the day easier, but I eliminate this option because I know my feet hate concrete walking. This leaves the third route, the preferred route in the guidebook. Adam posted about this route on Facebook, and from his descriptions, this slightly longer route is worth the effort, despite the intimidating climb leaving the city. The best part of making this decision is how confident I feel about my decision. I feel great about myself and my growing strength and stamina.

The path begins with a sharp right turn up a steep concrete sidewalk that immediately climbs above the rooftops. In a matter of minutes, I'm grateful it changes to senda path. Senda is the crushed gravel and makes my feet happy. The lushness of the landscape is different from the previous days of cultivated fields and wild, lush, flowering bushes. Today's landscape is filled with ferns, trees and outstanding mountaintop views of the city and river below. The gravel is a relief to my feet but does nothing for my lungs. I sound like a freight train.

The good news is, no one can hear me. With the exception of a father/daughter duo who pass me, I'm alone for over three hours, the time it takes to reach Trabadelo. When I arrive, my feet hurt, my bladder is near to bursting and I'm hungry as a bear. But, I've made it, still maintaining a perfect record on my intention to use indoor plumbing. It feels like I've already completed a full day's hike, but I know I still have two equally long distances to go before the day's end.

At the first open door I see, I stop. The front room of the alburgue Camino y Leyenda is warm and inviting. The room is enormous, serving as restaurant, office and coffee bar. Rugs decorate the tile floor. A wooden staircase leads to a second floor, and bright colors break up the darkness of the interior. There are hand-painted, inspirational messages hanging on both sides of the room. It feels like a home, complete with an adorable mixed breed puppy to entertain me.

In the center of this appealing atmosphere is a hospitalero with equally welcoming eyes and energy. I jettison my pack, order breakfast and painfully make my way up the stairs to use the facilities. I'm the only customer and receive celebrity service. My tortilla comes with lettuce and two large chucks of bread. Either the food is getting better each day, or my appreciation for it is increasing, because every breakfast tastes better than the last. I'm proud of my ability to meet the ups and downs of this morning's path and look forward to the next adventure. In spite of getting lost this morning, this has been the best day ever.

Refueled, recharged and raring to go, I set out to tackle the second hike of the day. There are three villages scattered along the 10.4 km to Herrerías, and I will use them to keep track of my progress. My goal in this second section is speed—to arrive as quickly as I can so that I'm in a position for success. While I hope to ride the horse through the third section, if I do have to walk the whole way to O'Cebreiro, a faster pace will help me get there before dark.

The road walking is not as bad as I thought it would be. The path runs next to the road. There isn't much traffic, and the countryside is beautiful. This portion of the Camino feels entirely different from this morning's walk. The flat surface lets me focus on speed, although no matter how quickly I walk, I continue to take time to capture images that inspire me. A sign in La Portela de Valcarce takes my breath away. It shows that I've walked 559 km since Roncesvalles, and I have another 190 km to go to reach Santiago. Wow!

I take a picture of another sign that's an advertisement for horses. I have another 6.5 km to go before reaching Herrerías, and the real question at hand is "Do I trust the Universe to supply me a horse, or do I call and make a reservation?" Right now, I'm trusting, but just in case I change my mind, I have the number in my phone. Not only is this a trust issue, it's a control issue, and even though I know what it is, it doesn't make it any easier. I really want to ride a horse up that mountain. Am I willing to give up CONTROL to the Universe? Do I REALLY believe my principles work? They have worked in the past, but will they work in this practical application? What if they don't work?

There is only one way to know for sure if I can manifest a horse, and I'm about to find out. My best bet is to trust and keep walking. The *whoosh, whoosh* of my pants legs sound like a metronome, a steady rhythm of motion propelling me forward. Arms, legs and walking sticks working in unison, moving like a well-oiled machine. I am a woman on a mission. I have a blind date with a horse.

Just past the sign indicating I have reached Ambasmestas, I see a couple soaking their feet in the cool running water of the canal. It's the perfect place to sit and soak. The water invites me to stop. I'm so tempted to soak my aching feet. But my inner voice won't let me. It urges me on, reminding me that if I want to ride, I better hurry.

Entering Herrerías, I wonder how I'm going to find the horses. I see a sign for a café a few hundred feet off the Camino and shuffle my way to it. I inquire about the horses in my less than stellar Spanish. The owners give me a blank stare, but a young customer takes pity on me and assures me, in English, that it's a small village, and I can't miss them. All I need to do is to follow the yellow arrows.

The village is quite small, and with each step I take, my heart rate increases. It's the moment of truth. So far, I haven't seen a single horse. I'm almost in tears. I guess if I don't find it, I will keep walking and steel myself for a tough climb. The road makes a gentle turn, and I see two horses in a pasture on the right. My heart skips a beat. Directly across the street, a man is sitting in a chair, eating an apple on a second-story balcony. He is wearing a bright green, short-sleeved shirt with a horse emblem, tan colored jodhpurs and sunglasses. Thick and wavy, graying hair tops his rail-thin body. My heart tells me that this is the place. I wave and ask, "Do you have a horse available to take me to O'Cebreiro?"

He asks, "When do you want to go?"

"How about ten minutes?"

"OK."

OMG! It was that easy. I've done it. I gave up control and trusted the Creator to manifest my desire. This is so exciting.

The horse wrangler's name is Victor, and he is very charismatic. After throwing his apple core into the pasture, he joins me at ground level. His English is excellent and we discuss price. I ask him about my backpack. He tells me I have a choice. I can ride with it on my back or transport it. It's very unappealing to think about balancing my pack, its weight pulling me backwards on the uphill climb. I want to enjoy this ride and don't want to fight with a heavy pack. It's also unappealing to be separated from everything I own. Darn it, there's that control issue again. I ask Victor questions about the transport service, and I'm sure he can tell that I'm uncomfortable with the idea of being separated from my pack. He suggests I go to the bar around the corner, enjoy a beer while he saddles the horses, and then decide what to do.

At the bar, I order a beer and ask the owner about shipping my backpack. For fifteen euros, she offers to have her mother deliver it for me, assuring me it will be waiting for me when I arrive. Her price sounds high, but I like the idea of knowing who has my stuff. I write my name and number, and the name of the hotel on a piece of paper. Using one of my safety pins, I attach the paper to the pack as a temporary nametag. After paying for the beer and the pack taxi, I sit back, enjoy the cold drink and celebrate the day. So far, it's been fantastic. The first leg was a magical solitary nature walk. I completed the second leg in record time. And the third leg makes my heart very happy. Last year I gave my horse, Pepper, to a friend's daughter so that Gerald and I could travel with greater freedom. It's been over a year since I've ridden, and I'm looking forward to being, as Gene Autry once sang, "back in the saddle again."

Returning to the stables, I'm surprised to see Victor is with two Pilgrims. Bob and Suyoung are newlyweds from Korea. Bob is a youth minister completing his second Camino. Suyoung is struggling on her first. We've seen each other before and greet each other in recognition. Victor is unable to get any more horses today and suggests Suyoung and I ride the horses, while he and Bob walk. I'm surprised by his suggestion, but quickly see the wisdom in his decision. He is a typical entrepreneur and just doubled his profit.

Bob and Suyoung eagerly agree to the plan. After completing our paperwork and putting on our safety helmets, we're ready to saddle up. They are typical horses for hire, acting like bored housewives, indifferent to our excitement. Mine is anticipation and joy. Suyoung's is fear; she has never ridden a horse before.

My steed is a huge bay mare named Coletta. With Victor's help, I mount and wait while he helps Suyoung. Normally I ride western but am comfortable on this English saddle. I'm very glad I shipped my backpack and look forward to an enjoyable afternoon. Poor Suyoung. Not only is she scared to death, her backpack is messing with her balance. She is the polar opposite of my comfort and looks very unhappy, but determined. I suspect, like me, she doesn't want to walk this section of the Camino. Her courage is impressive.

Following Victor's instructions, I give the universal "giddy up" signal to Coletta to take the lead. Unfortunately, Suyoung has no idea how to control her horse and allows it to lunge forward. Rather than fight a losing battle, we adjust. Victor grabs a hold of the tail of Suyoung's horse and allows it to drag him up the hill. Poor Bob walks behind us, trying to keep up under his own steam.

The trail is a mixture of gentle inclines interspersed with sections that feels like we're climbing stairs. Thank goodness the weather is perfect. This would be a scary ride in the rain. I was prepared for the steepness, but not the ruggedness of the trail. It reminds me of the hike into Molinaseca, the one that felt like I was walking on the bones of the earth. This time, I'm relying on the surefootedness of a horse. I do my part to make it as easy on her as possible. Leaning forward, I lay the reins on her neck and let her pick her way up the trail. She knows better than I the safest path to take up the trail.

I didn't look at the map before we left, so when we reach the first village, I think we have arrived. It's been a tough climb for my horse. I can't imagine walking it. It feels like we've gone farther than we have. I'm shocked to discover we're less than half way to our destination. At the Pilgrim font, we stop to let the horses cool off and drink their fill. Coletta is covered in sweat and blowing hard between deep sips of cool water. While we're waiting for the horses to satiate their thirst, I'm amazed to see Bob top the hill and join us. He's huffing and puffing, but by golly he made it. Just in time to watch us leave. Unlike Victor, Bob doesn't have a horse tail to propel him forward, and he quickly lags behind. We stop in the next village to allow the horses to drink again. Victor hasn't broken a sweat and isn't even breathing hard.

"How many times do you walk this trail?" I inquire.

"One to two times a day, several days a week."

Yep, that explains his whippet thin body and extraordinary endurance.

The horses aren't as thirsty as before and our break is rather short. Bob is nowhere in sight. Suyoung is concerned, but Victor assures her that he will make it. On the other side of Laguna de Castilla, we enter the Galicia Region. We have crossed a threshold of sorts. I'm in the same region as Santiago and feel like I've entered the homestretch.

We're literally on top of the world. We've reached the peak of the mountain and can see forever. Victor suggests we stop and offers to take our picture with the panoramic view behind us.

Now that we're on level ground, he leads us beside the rock wall until we reach the edge of O'Cebreiro where there are three horses already patiently tied to trees. Stiffly, I dismount while Victor helps Suyoung to the ground. He ties up the horses next to the waiting trio of horses.

The first people I see are Becky and Dale. They hiked up the hill and have already showered. I swear they must transport themselves from place to place. We invite Victor and Suyoung to join us for a cold beer, but Suyoung heads to her alburgue to wait for Bob. It took the horses over two hours to carry us up the mountain. I suspect it will be awhile before Bob shows up.

The rest of the afternoon is spent listening to Victor's tales and personal perspective on Galicia, Spanish history and the Camino. He introduces us to a new beer, 1906, and regales us with its heritage. To say that Victor is a proud Spaniard would be an understatement. We clap for Bob upon his arrival and continue to enjoy an afternoon of sunshine and breeze, laughter and stories. I experience my first taste of a Galician octopus specialty, *pulpo a la galega*. I'm not much of a fish eater, but I do love lobster and escargot, so I give the dish a try. It's yummy and a nice snack to hold me until dinnertime.

After checking into my hotel, I'm reunited with my bag and feel silly about my earlier control issues. I have enough time for a quick nap and hot shower before meeting Becky and Dale for dinner. This is Dale's second Camino and he serves as our fifteen-minute tour guide of this tiny village. Its location, at the top of the mountain, makes it one of the oldest villages built to serve Pilgrims. We skip the trinket shops to visit one of the oldest churches on the Camino; its beginnings date back to the 9th Century. Next to the church, we stop at the Don Elias Valiña Sampedro gravesite to honor his contribution to the Camino. He was a parish priest who introduced the yellow arrow to the Camino to assist modern Pilgrims. The impact of his idea is astounding. More than 200,000 people each year rely on those arrows to find their way to Santiago. Because of this man's passion, and his simple solution, I'm standing here today. Silently, I thank him.

After a delicious meal, we discover a shared enjoyment of Baileys and order a round. We have so much to share, so much to learn from each other and so little time. We head to another café to enjoy a second round of Baileys, before calling it a day.

Back in my room, lying on my bed, listening to the quiet, I am filled with satisfaction and joy. Because it doesn't get dark until almost 10:00 pm, it's hard to go to sleep even though it has been a long day. It feels like I completed three days of effort in one. I think about Don Elias and his contribution to the Camino, and realize, *I am a better person for the effort I made today. Because I am a better person, I can make the world a better place.*

Trusting the Creator to manifest a horse was an amazing experience and validated my GRIPP Life™ formula. The horse ride up the mountain was the icing on the cake for a Camino filled with Ease and Grace. Barhopping with Dale and Becky at the top of the world was an unexpected bonus of fun.

Day 30

Stage 27 - O'Cebreiro to Triacastela
20.7 km (12.86 miles)

Between the uncomfortable bed and aching muscles from the horseback ride, sleep was elusive last night. I tossed and turned until 6:30 a.m. Peeking out the window, I see fog. It's cooler up here, so I'm back in my wool shirt and layers. Thanks to Dale, I can read better this morning. Before dinner last night, he performed surgery on my glasses, stabilizing the hanging lens, pulling it higher. With the trifocal higher and closer to the top, my eyes don't hurt as much to use them.

According to my guidebook, today's elevation is fairly flat, until it drops off at the end of the day. Compared to the past two days, it looks like a piece of cake. I only have 20 km to walk today. Whoop! Whoop! Dale and Becky are headed to Triacastela too, so we have already made plans for dinner tonight.

By 7:30, I'm out the door and leaving O'Cebreiro's lofty views behind me. It's so foggy the Pilgrim in front of me quickly disappears into the mist. I'm walking in a cloud. There's nothing to see and nothing to look at except the shrubs and flowers lining the path, and a few feet of visibility. The longer I walk, the cloudier it gets. The lack of visual stimulation shifts my focus inward, to a landscape of internal dialogue. Before I left Texas, I knew I would come home a different person; I just didn't know who. During the weeks prior to the trip, Gerald and I laughed and questioned, "I wonder who WILL come home from the Camino?"

The wide, gentle, downward slope leads to deeper and deeper questions. There are so many pinging around the inside of my brain. What am I going to speak about in my NSA-NT showcase when I get home? What more can I do to support my brother in prison? Can I really write a book about my story that will help others? Do we sell the house in Boerne and pay off our debt? Do we sell the commercial real estate and simplify our life? If we do sell the house, where will we live? I love the beach, but do I really want to live there? How will these decisions affect the rest of the family? My girls are going through tough times while I'm walking the Camino. It has been satisfying to watch them face their challenges with courage and competence. Without Mom to hold their hand. I am so proud of them. Is this why my parents traveled so much when I was their age? Hmmm. So many questions with no easy answers.

On the other side of Linares, a giant bronze medieval Pilgrim statue rises from the mist from the other side of the road. The Pilgrim is hunched into the wind, hand on hat to prevent it from blowing away.

The statue perfectly reflects how I'm feeling right now. I trudge across the street to take a closer look, hoping to capture this mystical experience on my camera. According to the sign, this place is called Alto do San Roque. I'm standing at 1270 meters high. I'm not sure how high that is in feet, and don't really care, it won't make it warmer. It was 90 degrees a few days ago, and now it's cold enough to warrant gloves. I am grateful that I didn't ship my gloves to Santiago and dig them out of the bottom of my pack before heading on.

By the time I reach Hospital de la Condesa, I'm cold, wet, hungry and running out of energy—so much for my easy day. I pass an impressive stone church, with an open iron gate welcoming me to take refuge from the rain on its tiny porch. The ceilings, walls and floor are all stone. A bright, cheery green door is directly opposite from the gated entry. Masterfully crafted arched openings on both sides provide light in this manmade cave. Although a bit breezy, I've found a place to escape from the rain to enjoy my breakfast. It doesn't matter that the bread on my cheese and tomato sandwich is stale and crunchy; it's delicious and filling. Some fruit and a cookie round out the meal. I'm feeling better, and take my place among the parade of Pilgrims trudging through the rain.

After passing through Padornelo, the path takes an ugly turn. The temperature continues dropping and the incline of the path increases. *Wait a minute, what's going on? Why didn't the map show this?* Today was supposed to be downhill, not this hard climb. I'm not sure if it's the unexpectedness of the hill, the weather or my swirling thoughts that have me out of sorts. I do know how to master it. Twelve steps and a breath. Twelve steps and a breath. Put the poncho on when I'm cold, and take it off when I get overheated. All I have to do is keep going. Eventually, I will make it to the top. The final push is the most difficult. Popping out at the top of the hill, I'm relieved to see a café and quickly drop my bag outside to head indoors. The interior is toasty warm, thanks to a roaring fire in the fireplace. I take my time over a glass of fresh-squeezed orange juice and roll my feet under the table. A quick trip to the loo, and I'm ready to face the rest of the day.

Since arriving in Galicia, the architecture of the buildings is different, and for some reason, the villages today have been full of cow poop. These Spanish cows seem to have a bad case of diarrhea, and I do my best to avoid stepping in the splashes of green slimy goop. I've been around cows before, and know they smell, but have never tiptoed through a river of green poo before. Whew! The smell is obnoxious. I breathe through my mouth, which only slightly reduces the intensity of the stench.

Although it hasn't been that far since my juice break, by the time I reach Fonfría, I'm ready to warm up again. The Alburgue A Reboleria is a modern building, a welcome beacon among its medieval surroundings. The place is packed with Pilgrims chatting, enjoying food and drinks, and I suspect, like me, escaping for a moment from the stinky smell of cows. A hot chocolate and slice of Santiago cake are just what I need to reenergize.

It's noon and Fonfría is more than halfway to Triacastela. According to my map, the rest of the day is downhill with a red exclamation mark on my guidebook between Biduedo and Filloval. I hope the rain doesn't make the path too slippery. I will take my time on this dangerous section of the Camino.

Today is cow day. They are everywhere. I pass a man and his dog prodding and directing a small herd of cows up the road. Farther down the path, a huge bull, ring in nose, is sticking his face into the path, over a thick rock wall, to nibble the flowers on the other side. Pilgrims have lined up to take pictures and warily reach out to touch his face. Despite his massive size, the bull looks like a gentle giant. Hopefully I will have access to Wi-Fi tonight, so that I can text Kim for the symbolism of the cow. It's so dramatic how they showed up today.

As the altitude declines the weather improves. My concern for the red exclamation marked section of the path is replaced with relief. The Camino is busy today. I'm walking in a steady stream of Pilgrims who pass me with ease. A few have been very entertaining. A short-haired, stoutly built woman is actually jogging down the hill. Her backpack is flapping up and down to the rhythm of her steps. I don't know how she isn't falling down from its impact on her back. I suspect she's military or ex-military by her ability to charge down the hill.

A tiny woman in a bright blue poncho passes me too. She has a brown purse flung around her neck backwards so that it rests on top of her huge maroon backpack. Her plastic wrapped bedroll mat is tied to the bottom of her backpack and is hitting her on the back of her legs. She has plastic bags tied around her shoes, and despite her heavy load and makeshift rain gear, she is leaving me in her dust. I wonder why everyone is in such a hurry. I say a prayer of gratitude that I have time to enjoy myself, and continue down the hill in my unhurried pace.

The day is getting better by the minute, turning into a beautiful spring day. As I near Triacastela, I can feel the energy of the ancient roadway transporting me in time when there were three actual castles in the area, hence the name. Magnificent, mature trees line the path, protecting me from the now sunshiny day. Flowers are bursting with color at my feet, and my beloved cuckoo bird is singing. Texas weather is known to change in a minute, but this transformation has been incredible to experience. I have the energy to keep going, to walk past Triacastela, but I have a dinner date with friends. This is a journey to savor and I slow my pace even more to extend my time on the trail. I'm in no hurry for this beautiful nature walk to end.

By 2:30, I'm in my room with time to wash clothes, email Richard and see if Kim is available to send me the meaning of these cows. After restocking my food for tomorrow's journey, I have my response from Kim. There are so many meanings to consider.

Email to Richard:

So glad you received the post card! I picked one with lots of pictures for you to enjoy.

Today started off 30 degrees colder than last three days. Back in gloves, wool shirt and poncho for rain. Dropped about 2,000 ft. in altitude and the sun came out this afternoon.

Thom and Jodi (you sold him a car-he's my artist friend from Boerne) are meeting me tomorrow and walking last 100 km with me.

One more week to go.
Love you

PART THREE

Walking with Friends

"The whole of the holy life is good friends."

—The Buddha

Day 31

Stage 28 - Triacastela to Sarria
18.7 km (11.62 miles)

My best sleeping last night was between 1:00 to 5:30. My legs hurt today more than yesterday, which is surprising, considering the short distance. I have lots to think about while massaging the kinks out of my muscles this morning. Today is a BIG DAY, the day to meet Thom and Jodi. Time is so funny. Each day of walking is long, but each day is like a pearl on a pearl necklace, similar in size and shape, but when examined closely, each one is unique. The days run together, and it seems like it was only a few days ago since Thom and Jodi confirmed they were coming to meet me.

In some ways it feels incredible that I'm on target to meet them, and in others, it makes total sense. I expected my formula to work, and it has in wondrous ways. Walking in Faith isn't easy. I pushed past comfort zones and discovered I was capable of more than I thought possible. In the process, my self-esteem and confidence have grown. And, tomorrow everything changes. On the cusp of this change, I am feeling mixed emotions.

When I invited Thom and Jodi to join me, I had no idea how much I would enjoy walking on my own. I'm honored they accepted the invitation to travel halfway around the world to join me, and I'm looking forward to sharing this adventure with them. But I'm unsure if walking with them will change my experience. Torn between solitude and the joy of sharing this incredible experience is my new Camino.

It feels like the start of a third Camino. The first Camino was discovery of my "sea legs" and companionship with Sheelagh and Dennis. This second Camino has been a solitary challenge to meet a deadline, with a Dale and Becky dinner nightcap. Ironically, I've come all this way, learned so much about myself and still have not begun the "official" Camino. It has all been extra mileage, or "lagniappe" as my Louisiana friends would say.

It makes me laugh when people make negative comments about my deviation of accepted Pilgrim behavior. My life isn't about suffering, it's about living with joy, prosperity and fulfillment, no matter what happens. Why should my Camino be any different? Neither has to be hard, in my book. While some people feel the need to judge and criticize me, others have thanked me for giving them the courage to walk their Camino, their way. The reality is, neither matters because happiness is an inside job, independent of other people's opinions, unfavorable or favorable.

By 6:40 a.m., I'm out the door and realize I need an instant clothing adjustment to protect me from the light rain and early morning cold temperature. Before taking two steps, I see a man through the mist walking towards me. He looks relieved to see me and asks, "Do you know the right way to go? I'm lost." There is a choice of paths today. Because of my eyeglass situation, I've already looked at my map and know which way to go. At least I think I do.

Robert is from Ireland, and I'm pretty sure he thinks I'm a genius. He missed the turn on a prior attempt to find his way, looped around the block and ran into me while I was putting my poncho and gloves on. We enjoy the "new Pilgrim, nice to meet you" conversation. At the first small village we take turns taking pictures for each other. It's nice to have someone to take my picture with the countryside behind me; selfies by myself are no fun.

It doesn't take long to see that my pace is killing his soul, so I encourage him onward, reminding him that we're apt to run into each other again. We take a selfie together, then he lopes up the trail. I'm so happy to document the faces of the souls who I've enjoyed on this journey. Although Robert and I didn't spend much time together, our conversation was rich and rewarding. Chit-chat isn't the norm on the Camino. It's conversations about topics that really matter, even between strangers.

Robert is long gone and I have the trail to myself again. The woods today are hauntingly beautiful. Moss has turned brown trunks green, adding an additional layer to the emerald forest. Spring leaves, trunks and ferns fill the forest floor. I imagine fairies flying above the trees with wands turning everything green. Even the gray rocks have lichen growing on them. The only sounds are birds, waterfalls and the *whish-whish* of my pants.

On a rise, to the left, my eye is drawn to a red Coke machine and a green trashcan sitting in the middle of a small clearing. It's a surprise in the midst of this beauty, and I'm confused on its location. It looks and feels like a mistake, so I hurry past this disruption of natural serenity.

Ancient rock walls line the path on both sides. This must be part of the original route, because I can feel the energy of early Pilgrims here. I'm walking on rocks that feel like the earth's backbone again and take my time navigating the narrow trail. There's something special about walking on these giant slabs, stepping on the footprints of those who've come before, drawing me to the very center of the earth. On this holy space, bridging the gap through time and space to become one.

Nearing Sarria, I see a group of small children wearing tiny backpacks walking the Camino. Their riotous colors of pink, blue, green and yellow make them easy to spot from a distance. This is the first time I've seen a group like this, but I'm not surprised. I've been "warned" that from Sarria the Camino will be crowded with people. Many will be locals walking the final 100 km to earn their compostela.

I don't have to be fluent in Spanish to know what is going on; these children are being taught about the Camino by walking it. As I draw closer, I step to the street so that I don't have to pass through the pack of tiny tots. At last, I've found someone who walks slower than me! As I draw near, I hear one of the leaders say, "Buen Camino" and "Peregrino." In unison, the entire group of children, in typical childish sing-song voices, yell, "Buen Camino!" and wave. Tears sting my eyes and my heart melts. I AM a Peregrino.

By 12:30, I'm in Sarria with plenty of time to spare. My hotel is off the guidebook grid, so I stop at the visitor's center to pick up a map and directions. Siesta has begun by the time I arrive, and it takes several attempts to rouse anyone at the hotel. After a five-minute conversation, with my heart beating wildly, my reservation is confirmed. Whew, thank goodness! I'm escorted to the third story of this modern building. Our room has a laminate wood floor, three twin beds and an easy chair. The walls are painted a warm yellow, and two large windows overlook the river below. After a quick shower, I wash my stinky clothes then head out to the patio to watch them dry in the sunshine and digest the accomplishment of being here.

Deep in thought and warmed by the afternoon sun, I'm surprised when Thom and Jodi find me on the patio. Big hugs all the way around. We celebrate this union—we made it! My clothes are dry enough, so we head back to the room to catch up and make plans for the evening. They need to find a bank, and Jodi wants to find an art store. I need to find the cathedral to buy another credential, and last night I made plans to meet Dale and Becky for dinner. I'm thrilled to introduce these two lovely couples. I know they will enjoy each other, and for me, it feels like two sides of my life coming together—Before the Camino Cindy melding with Camino Cindy.

Tonight may be my last meal with Dale and Becky. They will follow the Brierley guidebook and arrive in Santiago on May 20th. Thom, Jodi and I will arrive the next day. In Rabanal del Camino, when I made reservations for the three of us, I remembered my first day and scheduled a short 10-km walk for tomorrow. Although Thom and Jodi have been preparing for this trip, I know a day to acclimate will help make the journey more enjoyable.

Another major advantage of our schedule, we will be out of sync with the majority of other Pilgrims. By starting each day, mid-section of the Brierley book, I expect to continue to enjoy quiet and tranquil mornings on the Camino. Despite warnings of crowding and trash between Sarria and Santiago, I intend to continue my Camino of Ease and Grace. After a short first day, we will walk four regular days, followed by a final short day. This will put us into Santiago in time to enjoy the noon Pilgrim mass.

After finding a bank to replenish our cash, we tromp around Sarria in search of an art store, grocery store or any store that sells pens. God love Thom, he is traveling with twin Geminis. Jodi's and my birthdays are two days apart. We are similar in that we don't let anything stop us from reaching a goal. Today, Jodi is determined to find an art store to purchase pens to decorate the plain khaki hat she purchased for this trip. As an artist, she is itching to spice up the blank canvas that her hat provides. Despite my aching feet, I enjoy participating in the hunt. After several unsuccessful attempts, Jodi snags some pens. They're not exactly what she wants, but will make do. There aren't a lot of options during siesta.

Next, we hike to the cathedral so I can buy a new credential. Without it, I can't obtain my compostela, which is pretty ironic given the effort I've made to get here. I forgot about siesta though, duh. Other Pilgrims have gathered and an informal line has formed. Rather than lose my place by leaving and coming back, I wait until the cathedral opens in thirty minutes, or so. I have an irrational fear that if I lose my place in line I may not get what I need.

And then I realize, it's not an irrational fear, it's my norm. I have lots and lots of practice of waiting my turn. As often as I could, I've stood in line for hours at a time for a chance to visit Richard at the prison. Before he was incarcerated, I never once considered what it is like for inmates and their families. I never knew the mass number of children who go in and out of prisons to visit their daddies. Until I joined them.

Just about anything can derail a visit, and even though, as an adult, I can understand why we're turned away after waiting for hours, I share the children's hurt when it happens. It always feels like I've won the lottery when I see Richard, and then again, when I make it back to my car. I've learned to wait with a grateful heart in uncertain situations. It is a useful skill I have used many times, like today.

When it's my turn, I'm confused by the volunteer. He wants me to buy two credentials. I question him, and he holds up his finger, indicating that I should wait. He heads to the back office and returns with a laminated card and reads from the card in English. I still don't understand, but for a few extra euros I get what I came for, plus one. Just in case he is right, that for some reason I don't know, I really DO need two credentials, I'm willing to play his game.

We have time for a beer before meeting Dale and Becky, so we wander down to the Camino, settle in our chair in front of an inviting café, just in time to reunite with the lovely French couple. A few minutes later, Tanja trudges by, sees me and squeals in delight. She still has a way to go today but takes time to join us for a cold one. Thom and Jodi are all smiles and seem to be enjoying the Camino, so far.

Our dinner date is just around the corner. Dale recommended

we meet at the Matías Locanda Italiana restaurant at 7:00 p.m. He ate here on his last Camino and has fond memories. The food is tasty, especially the pizza.

After an evening of enjoyable food and company, we say goodbye to Dale and Becky. The next time we will see each other will be in Santiago! They're planning to wait for us the next day and join us for Pilgrim mass at noon. I realize I left my jacket in the restaurant, and race back to pick it up. As I'm leaving the restaurant for the second time, I hear someone call my name. There is Robert, from this morning, grinning from ear to ear. My day has come full circle.

Day 32

Stage 29 - Sarria to Morgade
12.1 km (7.52 miles)

Thom snores. Every time I woke up last night and did leg exercises, Jodi was awake and waved "hi." We're more alike than I thought. Somewhere along the way, I must have slept, because I wake up to the light on. Thom and Jodi are packing their bags. According to Jodi, I snore too. She declares the Thom/Cindy symphony was pretty spectacular last night.

I'm a bit nervous about walking together and have said more than once, "This is your Camino and you need to walk it your way." Thom looks confused when I say it. I know it's hard to understand until you actually walk the Camino. *Could it be I'm giving myself a pep talk?*

Since walking with Sheelagh, I've copied her idea to take a picture each morning of the place I slept last night. Today is more fun because it includes a selfie of the three of us with the hotel in the background.

There are several pleasant surprises today. For starters, the trash is no better or worse than I've seen. Since leaving Sarria, we keep seeing strange-looking brick buildings sitting on stilts. They're long and narrow, bricks aligned to allow air to flow through the building, and decorated in various styles. Some are painted bright colors; others look almost like a religious shrine. They are so narrow that I would have trouble squeezing in. I have no idea what purpose they serve and I'm intrigued.

The countryside continues to enchant. My earlier concerns of walking together seem unnecessary. Thom and Jodi are easy to be with, and it's delightful to share this experience with them. It feels more like a stroll than a hike for me. They, on the other hand, seem to be struggling with the weight of their packs. I'm double glad I remembered my first day and scheduled a short walk for them today. Thom and Jodi have different walking styles, and I fit somewhere in between. Thom has settled into a pace of walking twenty minutes, then resting twenty minutes. Jodi walks fast. I struggle to keep up with her, but then she/we stop to wait for Thom. His pace is a killer for me, because every time I stop, I have to restart. Oh, those restarts. Until my feet warm up again, I hobble from the pain of walking on glass. I do better with continuous movement instead of this stop, rest, restart.

After several hours of strolling, my bowels are begging for relief. I leave Thom and Jodi resting in the shade of a forest and quick-step down the trail. Just around the corner, I'm relieved to see a busy alburgue. I throw my pack down outside, wait my turn in line to buy orange juice and ask about the restroom. I'm appalled to learn it's an outhouse—named "Casa Blanca"—in front of the café. *Great.* After waiting my turn in front of Casa Blanca, I discover there's no toilet paper. My emergency stash is in my backpack, so I have to return to the café to request toilet paper. *Great.* As if one trip to the outhouse wasn't enough for my humbling, I get to make two trips in front of all the Pilgrims sitting in front of the café. No secrets here.

I have no idea how long my Casa Blanca visit has taken, and don't know if Thom and Jodi have passed the café or not. I head down the trail, now in a hurry to catch up with them. After thirty minutes of fast walking, still no Thom and Jodi. Now, I wonder if they're still behind me. After finding a nice place to rest, I sit down and set my clock for ten minutes. If they don't come past in ten minutes, I'll assume they're ahead of me and keep going. They don't have a map, but I did give them the name of our hotel, so they should know where to go. At the end of ten minutes, the alarm on my phone rings, and no sign of Thom and Jodi. I call Jodi, but no answer. *GREAT. I'VE LOST THEM ON THE FIRST DAY!*

By the time I reach the 100-km marker, I feel confident they're ahead of me. I wait my turn for a big group of Pilgrims to take lots and lots of pictures together, and ask one to take my picture at this momentous occasion. Wishing Thom and Jodi were here to enjoy this "official" start of the Camino with me, I call Jodi again and she answers. I haven't lost them. In fact, they've already reached tonight's destination and are waiting for me. Sigh.

Knowing they are OK, I can relax and enjoy my time here, alone. In doing so, I realize I've taken on responsibility for them, without their permission, or request. I am not their caretaker, nor do they want me to be. With this awareness I can let go of feeling responsible for them. My heart breathes a sigh of relief.

When I arrive around 12:30 our room isn't ready yet. Thom and Jodi are sitting on a bench, enjoying the scenery. We move to chairs in front of the casa rural, catch up on the highlights of the day and watch the Pilgrim traffic pass. My body appreciates the short walk. It feels almost like a rest day to me. While we're waiting, one of the bag transportation services pulls up in front of us to deliver backpacks to the casa rural.

Thom's eyes light up when he discovers he can ship his backpack for three euros per day and relieve himself of this heavy burden. He is suffering mightily from a blister on the bottom of his foot. He heads off to the front desk to inquire about shipping his backpack, especially since our daily distance will double for the next few days.

After our room is ready, we take turns taking showers, and Thom and Jodi lay down to rest. I head to the bar to catch up on my notes. I begin reading our next *Artist's Way* book, Finding Water, by Julia Cameron, while enjoying lunch and a cold beer. Tomorrow night's accommodations require me to confirm today, but every time I call, they hang up. After several attempts, I ask the Morgade casa rural owner to help me. He is a real character, very engaging, and after the lunch crowd is over, he's able to confirm our reservation for tomorrow night's lodging.

Later in the afternoon, I head to the front of the building to see if I recognize any fellow Pilgrims as they pass. I enjoy a delightful conversation with a new Pilgrim, and am honored when a black cat jumps in my lap to enjoy an afternoon nap in the sun. Another best day ever!

Day 33

Stages 29 & 30 - Morgade to Ventas de Narón
22.8 km (14.17 miles)

We tiptoe down the wooden stairway, leave Thom's backpack for pickup and step out onto the trail. It's not quite 6:45 and still dark, but we have a long way to go today so I'm anxious to get an early start. Thom is stepping gingerly, unsure if he'll be able to walk the entire distance today.

Last night after dinner, Jodi and I had very different opinions on how to treat his blister. If I hadn't recently gained a lot of blister care experience, I wouldn't have said anything, but as usual, anytime I get an ounce of expertise, I'm quick to share an opinion. In hindsight, I can see I should have stayed out of the conversation. Poor Thom, he was put in the awkward position of choosing his wife's treatment plan or the one that I proposed. It probably felt like sister wives, without the benefits.

The morning greeting from the cuckoo brings a smile to my face. I didn't hear any yesterday and missed them. I've never owned a cuckoo clock and never thought about buying one, but after this trip I might get one. Wouldn't it be magical if every time I heard the clock, it would bring me back to the Camino? But, then again, maybe I won't need the clock. My sense is this journey is being imprinted on my very soul, and I won't need any reminders.

Except for the three of us, the Camino is deserted. Mother Nature is showing off this morning with a magnificent, mystical sunrise. As the sky turns brighter, the landscape appears from the darkness. Mountain peaks rise above cloud-filled valleys, looking like islands surrounded by swirling lakes of white mist. Witnessing this miraculous moment with these two gentle spirits makes me happy, which is a pleasant surprise after the concern I felt in giving up my solitude.

Memories of the Grand Canyon trip with Gerald and his cousins flash across my mind, and I realize I shouldn't be surprised. The Grand Canyon trip taught me we can walk side by side and still have unique journeys. Somewhere along the way, I lost this awareness, until now. We may share the path, but we journey alone.

Just past Ferreiros, we stop for breakfast at Casa do Rego. The building is invitingly modern, but built with traditional materials, a style that appeals to me. Inside, I'm reunited with a table full of Pilgrim friends I've met along the way. Mike, Andre and Malcolm, who I last saw at the Parador breakfast table, are still together. And Hanna! I see her often and am fascinated by how she keeps popping up with various groups of different people. In addition, there are several other Pilgrims I don't know—yet.

While paying for our delicious breakfast, the owners tell us the story of how they met. Years ago, she met him walking the Camino, they fell in love, married and just opened this casa. Before we leave, they generously offer everyone a shot of lemon flavored liquor and salute our Camino. We leave with a smile on our faces and a fire in our full bellies.

Other than the assault to my nose from the stench of cows when we pass through villages, the day is near perfect. Not too hot, not too cold, no rain, and the fog has cleared. There is something new to see around every bend. Flowers, amazing vistas and those interesting tall and narrow buildings are in almost every yard. Walking with artists gives me a new perspective. Jodi sees patterns and shapes that I would have missed. We have a blast capturing them with our phone cameras.

Thom's day is slightly less perfect. Sending his backpack has helped, but I can see he hurts with each step he takes. Without the heavy pack, he has a chance of making it today, but his progress is slow. He urges Jodi and me to walk ahead, to enjoy our Camino. Although we hate to leave him, he knows where we're staying tonight, and I know that our departure will allow him to enjoy his Camino more. He won't have to worry about "keeping up" and can enjoy his day at his pace.

Jodi and I stop for a bathroom break and meet two new Pilgrim friends, Barbara and Jackie. One is from Louisiana and the other from Kansas. No spring chickens, these two spry ladies have been slowly making their way across Spain. Their most outstanding features are their smiles. I ask Jodi to take my picture with these two precious women. They have their own approach to walking the Camino. When the path is steep, they call a taxi. When they get tired, they rest. Some days, they only make three or four kilometers and are in no hurry to finish. It's all about the journey for Barbara and Jackie.

Planning the Camino is nothing more than managing the resources of time, energy and money. Barbara and Jackie are lucky. They have unlimited time and money to overcome their limitation of energy. Most people have at least one limitation, others have two, and some are limited by all three. Meeting Barbara and Jackie has been a gift; I'm not the only one walking the Camino with Ease and Grace.

By the time Jodi and I reach the bridge crossing the Rio Mino, we're hot and tired. Portomarín is approximately halfway to our destination, and a good place to rest and wait for Thom. According to Dennis, there are stairs leading to the water. He saw Pilgrims playing here on his last Camino and told me about them during our dinner in Molinaseca when I was lamenting about not being able to put my feet in the river. Dennis assured me I would have another opportunity in Portomarín. And, now it's here!

Jodi is always willing to play, so I'm confident she'll be willing to join me in the water. As we cross the bridge, I see the stairs and make my suggestion. After winding our way around the edge of the bridge, we wiggle through overgrown vegetation, bounce down the steps and plop our feet in the water as fast as we can remove our shoes and socks. The water is cool and soothing on our feet and legs.

While we're enjoying the water, we keep an eye out for Thom. With his bright green jacket, white hair and single walking stick, he's easy to spot crossing the bridge. Jodi and I stand up to yell and wave as he marches across the bridge. His concentration is so intense, I'm afraid we're going to fail to get his attention. He finally sees us and waves. We motion for him to join us. He makes his way down the stairs, removes his shoes and sighs in relief when his feet hit the cool water. I share Jodi's relief that he's made it this far. The three amigos are back together.

After air drying our feet, we squeeze our refreshed feet back into our shoes and climb the steep stairs that leads back to the Camino. We locate a grocery store to purchase food to carry in our pack. Then we wander to the town square for a lunch stop. It's a typical slow Sunday in Spain. The streets are barren. We find a bar that's open and order a round of beer. Thom urges Jodi and me to walk ahead. He's ready for lunch and in no hurry to move forward. Honoring his request and itching to go, Jodi orders a sandwich for the road. We urge Thom to take care of himself. We have another 12-km to go, and Thom has to figure out how to manage his energy and time resources.

Jodi and I set off for a girls-only adventure. Our afternoon is filled with a mixture of laughter, stories, silence and awe. We stop in the forest outside of Castromaior to refuel and rest. She generously shares her egg-salad sandwich when we break for lunch. We giggle as we lick the melting sandwich from our fingers and agree that it would have been safer and tastier if we had eaten it earlier. As Pilgrims pass, she offers them a cookie from the stash she purchased at the grocery store. There have been few stops to purchase food today, and it's fun to watch the passing faces change from surprise to appreciation.

It's 4:00 p.m. by the time we stumble to our destination. Ventas de Narón is a tiny village made up of two private alburgues. With the limited accommodations, I can see why the owners wanted us to confirm our reservation last night. At first sight, I'm relieved to see the open air patio and welcoming bar/restaurant facilities. Tables are filled with Pilgrims drinking beer and telling stories in various languages. Laughter fills the air and clothes blow in the brisk breeze.

After checking in, the hospitalera leads us out the backdoor of the beautiful alburgue to a metal building that is attached to a cow barn. Uh-oh. I'm pretty sure my face is giving me away, clearly showing the horror I'm feeling. The door opens to an entryway that has two rooms on each side, for a total of four private rooms. The bathroom door is directly across from the exterior door. We're given the keys to two rooms, side by side. Feeling terrible about our accommodations, I urge Thom and Jodi to pick the room of their preference, not that it makes much difference.

Oh, my goodness, we're sleeping in a cow barn tonight! We even paid extra to do so. WOW. Cow stench, up close and personal. With any luck, my nose will go numb soon. To cheer myself up, I tell myself that it's not too bad if the windows and doors are closed. I hope Thom and Jodi will forgive me for booking us in this stinking room.

After a quick shower, I head out to the patio to wash my clothes and hang them to dry. It's a little late to be doing laundry, but the wind is blowing hard enough, I think they'll dry before it's time to go to bed. It doesn't get dark until after 9:00, so there's plenty of daylight. If they don't dry, I'll pin them to my backpack tomorrow. Thom and Jodi stay in the room to rest, shower and catch up.

While my clothes dry, I enjoy a cold beer, write up my daily notes, then send Richard an email. When I open up the CorrLinks app on my phone, I discover my subscription will expire in a few days. CorrLinks is approved by the Federal Bureau of Prisons for inmates to communicate by email. There is a free version, but I like the paid version better, because it alerts me when I receive an email. The cost is minimal for the peace of mind I receive in knowing when Richard reaches out to me. The subscription renewal is an unexpected detail to deal with on the Camino, but I'm happy to update my account so that I don't lose contact with him.

To bring my phone, or not bring my phone, was a difficult decision to make. I flip-flopped several times before deciding to bring it. During the planning stage, I read a lot of verbiage about the "right" way to walk the Camino. At first, I was surprised by the pressure to conform to these Camino standards, but then I remembered the Camino is a metaphor for life. The rules of "proper" Camino behavior can be traced to its long and rich history. Unfortunately, modern Pilgrims are expected to follow this ancient rulebook, and Pilgrims who choose to ignore the rules are subjected to judgment and discrimination. The irony is the rules use outward behaviors to measure an internal journey, which makes them totally inadequate.

The phone decision was really a struggle about seeking the approval of others, a lifelong challenge for me. Once I recognized the real issue, it was easier to decide what to do. I mustered up the courage to boldly communicate my rule-breaking moments so that I could practice facing disapproval. My plan has worked beautifully. It's given me the opportunity to draw criticism, which has given me the opportunity to face my discomfort of receiving disapproving comments. Each time I'm ridiculed, I'm given the opportunity to grow, to seek my own approval.

The Camino is full of growth opportunities. Last night, when Thom and Jodi suggested I offload some of my stuff in a shipped backpack, I realized I still have control issues to overcome. My backpack has been comfortable since León, but I stretch myself and slip my pink stuff sack with my extra clothes in Thom's backpack. Ironically, my lighter pack causes my body to strain harder. I'm satisfied that I can give up control, but for the sake of my back, I will carry my own stuff going forward.

For my Pilgrim meal tonight, I order pasta as an appetizer, and gag on the first bite. Thom and Jodi have ordered the pasta as well and seem to like it. I tentatively take another small bite. Nope, still bad. It tastes like fishy fish, something I avoid at all costs. Confused, I ask if anyone else can taste it. Jodi agrees and thinks it's probably tuna. I knew the closer I got to Santiago and the coast, fish would become more prevalent. But I had no idea they'd sneak it into the pasta. Yuck.

After dinner, we head to our rooms and say goodnight. From my bedroom, through the walls, I hear fresh delivered cows mooing their protest and dogs shouting at them to shut up. Despite my earplugs, I drift to sleep to the lullaby of *moooooooooooooo, woof, woof, woof, mooooooooooooooo.*

Email to Richard:

No Internet last night, so I'm sending this from somewhere between Sarria and Melide. Thom and Jodi made it and I gave them your regards! I will complete this journey on May 21st!

From there, unsure of my plans.

Love you,
Cindy

Day 34

Stages 30 and 31 - Ventas de Narón to Melide
26.5 km (16.47 miles)

Today is Thom's birthday. I'm grateful that he and Jodi accepted my invitation to join me on this trip. In the invitation, I used words that he and Jodi wrote in their book, *Dare to Dream*, so basically, they inspired themselves to come.

Our day starts as usual, 6:45 am, and we're happy, happy, happy to say goodbye to our cow-barn lodgings. It's extremely foggy this morning, cool enough for my wool shirt. With limited visibility, we enjoy the lush green fields, spring flowers and yard art as we pass. I'm pleased and surprised that all the dire warnings of trash and crowded conditions have proved false. Once again, we have the Camino to ourselves.

In Ligonde, we enjoy a leisurely breakfast. But for me, it's a bit too leisurely. When Thom heads up to the counter for a second cup of coffee, I can't contain myself any longer, jump up to leave and murmur something about walking our own Camino. They have the Melide hotel name and we'll meet up tonight to celebrate Thom's birthday.

Two kilometers later, I see giant ant sculptures outside A Paso de Formiga alburgue and stop to take pictures. Inside, I use the facilities while my hot chocolate is being prepared. While I'm sipping on my hot frothy goodness, Jodi blows into the room, looking a bit shaken, which isn't her normal state. She explains that she left shortly after I did, to let Thom walk on his own. In the short distance between breakfast and here, a man in a car tried to get her into his car, twice. The man was insistent. She doesn't have her phone today, so she was unable to call me or Thom. She is very relieved to find me.

Needless to say, with the girl, Denise Thiem, still missing from April, this is quite upsetting. I've had no such issues on my journey, which makes me both happy and sad. Happy that I'm gray headed and stout as a mule. Sad that I'm not abduction worthy. When I do my standup comedy, I have a line that seems to be true. "No one wants to schlep their grandma." Apparently that includes abductors. Oh well, I can add it into my next routine.

When we return to the path, we keep our eyes peeled for the pervert in the white car, but I'm not concerned. Abduction doesn't fit into my Camino of Ease and Grace.

The day continues to be overcast and cloudy, which is fine by me. When Jodi isn't walking ahead of me, we walk side by side and make plans for Thom's birthday. When we reach our destination tonight, she wants to buy a cake and flowers to celebrate. I think she's crazy, but I'm willing to go along with her plan.

Her love and devotion for Thom inspires me. Their relationship is built on cherishing each other, and it shows in all their interactions. They have only been married a few years and were married on our ranch. They are some of the first people we met when we moved to Boerne, Texas, which coincided with the beginning of their relationship. I have watched their relationship develop, and in doing so, have followed their example by cherishing my relationships with my loved ones more.

After watching Jodi hunt for pens back in Sarria, I'm sure this afternoon will be similar; she will be relentless until she achieves her goal. The pens have been used every night to paint on her plain, khaki hat. Right before my eyes, she is creating a masterpiece. It's fascinating to see it evolve and change every night.

As the day unfolds, Jodi's "get up and go" is fading. One of her knees is aching, and she has developed a hitch in her giddy up. She seriously considers calling a taxi, but after the purchase of a knee brace and a few beer stops, she's able to keep going. By the time we reach Melide, it's 3:45. We're both tired and ready to be done walking for the day. Hotel Carlos isn't on the Camino. Reviewing the map, I think we can shave some distance off our day by taking a shortcut. After asking directions several times and not understanding any of the answers, we follow my gut and pop out across the street from our hotel. I proclaim my success, "Just like a bird dog!"

We're greeted at the hotel by a young man named Victor. He is the second Victor I've met in Spain who speaks excellent English. Jodi tells him her plan for Thom, and Victor says he can make all the arrangements. Viola! Birthday arrangements made with Ease and Grace. Love it, especially since we're both tired, and she's hurting.

Our room is very spacious and elegant. The floor is covered in gold and red patterned carpet. The windows have both sheers and drapes, and the three beds look comfy and inviting. There's even a bathtub in the bathroom. Yea-baby! Fifteen minutes later, Thom rolls in. He thoroughly enjoyed his solo journey and is covered in the Camino spirit.

I leave the lovebirds alone and head to the bar to catch up on my notes and communicate with family and friends. The bar matches the elegance of the room. Victor assures me the cake and flowers are on their way. I see a decadent chocolate cake and order a Bailey to go with it. Thinking of Dale and Becky, I wish they were here to enjoy this with me.

While eating my cake, I meet another Pilgrim couple. We're few and far between at this hotel, since it isn't on the Camino. After learning I started in St. Jean, they're hesitant to share their start point of Sarria. Fear of disapproval shows in their eyes. Little do they know, I know exactly how they feel. When I sincerely applaud them, they relax and thank me for my encouragement.

Thom and Jodi wave as they head out the door to explore the city. Jodi is taking him "pretend" birthday shopping so that he'll be surprised later with his cake and flowers. We plan to eat later at one of the restaurants Victor has recommended that serves *pulpo*, the regional specialty octopus dish. While they're gone, I head up to the room and enjoy a hot bath.

When Thom and Jodi return, they update me on tonight's plan. While taking their walk, they ran into a group of Pilgrims that Jodi and I met at one of our beer stops today. They want to celebrate Thom's birthday with us, so we're meeting them for dinner. When we arrive, there are seven other Pilgrims ready to celebrate.

The pulpo is delicious but the steak I order is rancid. I request the charge be removed from the bill, and the waiter agrees without hesitation. After the cake and Bailey snack, I wasn't too hungry anyway. One of the women in the party is obnoxious, drunk and demanding everyone pay the same amount towards dinner. I don't do well with people telling me what to do, or reaching into my pocketbook without permission. Since my dinner was zero, I offer 10 euros towards the shared appetizer and tip, which was generous on my part because I ate so little. She isn't happy, not so much about the money, as about not getting her way. Her husband does his best to settle her down. Out of the corner of my eye, I can see Thom and Jodi are enjoying the show.

When we return to the hotel, Jodi suggests we stop in the bar for a nightcap, but it's really a ploy to spring her surprise. Thom is all smiles when Victor presents the cake and flowers. A group of Spanish men sing "Happy Birthday" in Spanish. This is one celebration Thom will cherish forever. I'm thrilled to be a part of it.

Happy Birthday, Thom!

Email to Richard:

I'm 3 days away from completing this walk. The closer I get, the more unbelievable it is that I'm doing it.

Love you!

Is the Camino safe for women to walk alone?

Given Jodie's experience, I was compelled to include this safety tip for women.

On Easter morning, Denise Thiem was last seen leaving Astorga, Spain. Five weeks later, I followed in her footsteps with a sense of unease. As I passed her photo that blanketed the trees and lampposts, I kept my eyes peeled in vain and sent prayers for her safe return. Tragically, I learned after my trip, on September 11, her body was found, and the person responsible for her abduction was arrested.

Denise's disappearance created quite a stir. Other stories of near abductions, men masturbating on the trail and stalking began to surface. But when you consider that, according to the Pilgrims Welcome Office, more than 80,000 women complete the Camino each year, the Camino is one of the safest places on Earth.

The unfortunate truth is women have valid reasons for concerns of personal safety. We are targeted for violence because of our gender. But, we cannot let fear rule our lives. The greatest tragedy would be submitting to fear and missing your Camino.

We can't bring Denise back. But we can honor her memory by having the courage to walk our own Camino.

As women, we must protect ourselves. For me, that included setting my intention of Ease and Grace and listening to my Intuition. Some women walk in groups, others carry mace. What do you need to feel safe? How will you protect yourself? Honor yourself and do whatever it takes.

Buen Camino, Peregrina

Day 35

Stages 31 & 32 - Melide to Salceda de Caselas
Camino, 25.5 km (15.85 miles), lost on freeway, 6 km (3.72 miles) Total, 31.5 km (19.57 miles)

Thom, Jody and I decide to walk separately today, then make plans to meet tonight. It's 8:30 before I'm out the door. I'm so out of sync, I forget to take my morning photo in front of the hotel.

Finding my way to the Camino is a breeze, and I follow the arrows through town. In Santa Maria, I stop to take a photo of a beautiful palm tree, the first I've seen on the trail. Another sign of getting closer to the coast. There are few Pilgrims on the trail this morning. I'm ecstatic with the continued solitude, even though it means I have to wait awhile for someone to come along so that I can ask them to take my picture at the 50-km marker. My excitement is growing. It's amazing to be this close. I feel like super woman, except I traded my cape for a backpack.

Today is my grandson Christian's fifth birthday. I hope when he grows older he will appreciate the importance of this trip. *I love you, Christian, and I am sending my love to you in Spirit.*

The Camino quickly transitions into forest, and I'm blown away by the smell of eucalyptus. The trees are so tall, they block the light and engulf me in their embrace. As I walk, I hear a conversation between my heart and my dad. It's like I'm eavesdropping on their conversation.

"See Dad, I CAN finish what I start! Until I earned my Bachelors and Masters Degrees, you said I never finish anything."

"I know, baby, and I'm sorry. Until I made it to this side, I didn't understand that you are able to juggle one thousand balls at the same time. Please forgive me."

His words help me realize that judgment comes from a lack of understanding. Healing tears flow down my face as I continue to walk.

The next conversation is with my mom.

"Mom, why didn't you set a better example for me as a woman?"

"Cindy, my soul had its own agenda, and it didn't include setting an example for you. Remember, love, you picked me as your mother. Your soul has its own agenda. It's up to you to discover your own way, to embrace your genuineness and love yourself. It's why you're here."

I feel the ache, deep in my heart release, and continue to walk. The next conversation is with my body.

"Thank you for getting me this far with such little care. Thank you for holding my pain. Will you forgive me for all the abuse I've heaped on you?"

"Yes, Cindy, you are forgiven."

Stopping short, I bend over to catch my breath. I'm not the same person I was an hour ago.

In Boente, I stop at the alburgue for breakfast. The French omelet is the best food I've ever tasted. I don't know if it's really that good or if I'm still in an altered state. It really doesn't matter. The world is a brighter, happier place. As I enjoy my meal, I feel love, loved and loving. I'm raw, vulnerable and real.

After breakfast, I enter another forest and receive additional downloads. My intention in walking the Camino was to test my philosophies on life, and IF they worked, share them. But the Camino is teaching me a subtle difference. I can share my principles, but the real lesson is to encourage people to discover their own life principles, to test them and live them. Ahhhh!

Everyone needs to walk *their own* Camino. Duh. Double Duh.

And then, there is the truth. When I became a certified coach with John P. Strelecky last year, he introduced me to the idea that it only takes one data point to change the truth. Fears, past hurts and limiting beliefs have melted away on this journey. Or should I say, sweated away. I'll bet that's why I stink. My stinking thinking is coming out through my pores!

The conversations with my parents were special this morning, because I was able to talk to them directly. In the past, I hired Peggy Rometo, a psychic medium, to channel them. Peggy is a proven intuitive who volunteers with Find Me, a non-profit organization dedicated to locating missing persons and resolving homicides. For months, in the midst of my family crises, she connected me with my parents in real time. I didn't have to wonder what to do. I could ask them through Peggy. It was the most healing thing I did and the best money I spent. Better than the money I spent on attorneys, that's for sure. Talking with my parents after they passed was something only my closest, closest friends knew about. I wasn't ready to face judgment, ridicule or disapproval. I wasn't ready to defend myself. But now, I know it's important that I gather the courage to share. It might be the one data point that helps someone else.

I'm reminded of Arthur Schopenhauer's words of wisdom: "All truth passes through three stages. First, it is ridiculed. Second, it is violently opposed. Third, it is accepted as being self-evident." Someday, I pray, it will be accepted as self-evident that death is not the final answer. Truth is a belief, held in a specific place and time, that changes with additional information. When we're open and flexible to a changing truth, we can stop fighting about it. Everyone has their own truth. Peace comes when we allow others the right to their own truth.

In Casa Calzada, I stop for a beer and gather my thoughts. I feel like my line in the sand was drawn today, and no matter how uncomfortable I am, or how unacceptable they are to society, I can't hide my truths any more. Contrary to what I was taught in school, Christopher Columbus was not the first person to believe the world was round. The idea of a spherical earth was proposed by Eratosthenes of Cyrene, who lived from 276 to 194 BC. BC! He not only calculated the Earth's axis and circumference, he invented the Leap Day and created the first map of parallels and meridians. His ideas are wildly accepted today, but back in 1492, when Columbus sailed to America, society still believed the world was flat. Yep, truth takes time to be accepted by the masses.

One of my fellow Toastmasters once gave a speech on how long it takes to reach one million people. What took centuries, now takes minutes or seconds; I don't remember the exact figure.

All I know is now the amount of time it takes to reach people has been DRASTICALLY reduced. Let's hope the time it takes for the truth about the afterlife and creating our own reality will pass its way quickly to mainstream beliefs.

The trail between Casa Calzada and Salceda is a delightful natural path. But it's been a long day, over 25 km. When the path drops down to the freeway, I see a shortcut to the hotel. My bird dog skills worked like a charm yesterday. I'm looking forward to an early arrival today. It's only 2:30 and I'm almost home for the night. Whoop! Whoop!

According to my map, the hotel should be just to my left. Walking next to the freeway is a whipping. The back draft from trucks blows so hard that I have to stop, turn away from the road and brace myself for the wind that follows. The hotel isn't where it's supposed to be. I wonder, for just an instant, if I should go back to the Camino. Dismissing the thought, I check the map again, guess I haven't gone far enough, so I keep going. And going. And going.

Something is terribly wrong.

I see a bar up ahead with a van in front. I hurry to ask the driver about my hotel location. He points in the direction I came, but I can't understand what he's saying. Boy, it sure would be helpful to understand Spanish at times like this. I head back down the freeway to my starting point. From the mile markers, I know I've put an extra 6 km of freeway walking in and still haven't arrived at my hotel.

Rather than return to the Camino, I stubbornly keep going and soon see my hotel. Pilgrims are crossing the freeway right next to it. Groan. My bird dog skills certainly failed me today. My little shortcut added an extra hour. By the time I check in, it's almost 4:00. My nerves are shot. After the transformational walk this morning, I am humbled by the extra mileage this afternoon. I wonder, *What is my lesson in this?*

Day 36

Stages 32 & 33 - Salceda de Caselas to Lavacolla
18 km (11.18 miles)

By the time Thom and Jodi made it in last night, I had taken a shower, sent my clothes to be washed and dried and made a new friend from New Mexico. Like Thom and Jodi, Lena is an artist and the three of them really hit it off during dinner. Thom and Jodi are planning to travel to Portugal after the Camino. They have invited me to join them. As much as I enjoy traveling with them, I'm ready to go home. Lena has rented a house in northern Spain for the month of June. She invited Thom and Jodi to join her. Knowing them, it will probably happen.

Today we're only walking, 18 km, which is 10 km shorter than yesterday. Since breakfast is included in the cost of the room, we delay our departure to eat when the doors open at 7:00. The interior is ultra-modern, but the building itself is made of stones. It's another good example of architecture blending old with the new. Food is laid out buffet style, but the owner serves us since we are one of two tables that are occupied. He even offers to take our picture.

We're ready to go by 8:30, just as it starts to drizzle. Jodi and I don our ponchos and pretend we're Igor from the movie *Young Frankenstein*. Thom takes our picture goofing around and we burst out in giggles.

We take the alternative path to the Camino and drop onto the

N-547, which is only slightly less busy than the freeway I walked next to last night. The difference is this is the Camino and there is an actual path to walk on, even if it is next to the road. Last night, I was the lost idiot hiking a major freeway. If I'd been in Texas, I would have been arrested for being bat-s#it crazy.

It takes an hour to cover the first 4 km. We stop for a fresh juice and a bathroom break at the O Ceadoiro Restaurante. Sitting at the table, I review the morning's photos. There is the new white Mercedes parked under the rickety wooden shed, a chicken that looks like it's dancing, flowers and a bright colored green door. The surprises continue around every curve. I've loved capturing these memories. Oh, there's also the *horreo*. Horreos are the long narrow buildings built on stilts that I've been wondering about since Sarria. Apparently, they are the unofficial symbol of Galicia and used as granaries to dry produce. Humph, learn something new every day.

We have the entire patio to ourselves and have seen few Pilgrims on this section of the trail this morning. According to the map on the wall, we're only 23 km from Santiago. Whoa! I could easily make that distance today. Then it strikes me. *What's the rush?*

The closer I get, the less I want the journey to end, just like life. The older I get, the more I appreciate the time I have remaining. This realization hits me like a ton of bricks. Everything SLOWS down. It feels like my entire system has gone into slow motion to capture each sight, sound, smell, taste and feeling in the moment. The Camino is life, and Santiago is Heaven.

I know Dale and Becky will be there to greet me. And others, who will surprise me. They will celebrate my arrival, and I bet we immediately begin planning a return trip together. Yes, today is a day to savor. Each bird call, each laugh and each misty moment.

After a loop around the airport, we reach our destination by 2:30. Thom is hurting and my legs are aching a bit. We check in to our room, wash our laundry and hang our clothes in the window to dry. Jodi pulls out paint and brushes. Ironically, she lost her hat yesterday and didn't even know it until it was returned to her. Another Pilgrim found it and retraced his steps to find her. I love the Camino!

The hat is no longer khaki colored. She has painted the Camino on it. A Camino shell is front and center. Around the sides, she's captured the Eucalyptus Forest, the up and down of the trail, and even the bicycle rider that almost hit us. Jodi asks Thom and me for words that describe our trip and adds them to the edge of the brim. Then she asks us to sign it. WOW, she is so talented. What a gift to be able to capture the journey on a hat.

At dinner, we reconnect with one of the couples from last night's dinner fiasco. The restaurant is ultra-fancy, the food delicious. Back at our room, it's lights out, with the realization that TOMORROW WE REACH SANTIAGO!

Email to Richard:

I will arrive in Santiago tomorrow to attend the Pilgrim mass by noon.

It's been quite the journey. I feel like you have been on it with me. Thank you for being my brother.

I love you.
Cindy

Day 37

Stage 33 - Lavacolla to Santiago de Compostela
10.2 km (6.34 miles)

According to the map, it looks like we are in a suburb of Santiago, so I know the day will be concrete walking. We're in no hurry because we only have ten tiny kilometers to go today. Even though we are so close, there are forest and green pastures to enjoy before the hustle and bustle of the city. At the top of the hill, Monte del Gozo, we take a few minutes to enjoy the view of the city of Santiago sprawled out below us. We enjoy the Del Gozo monument and fight the urge to buy trinkets from the dealers that have set up below the statue.

There are so many interesting things to see. It is a day of eye candy for my artist friends. Nothing is skipped. From more horreos, the eucalyptus forest, ancient church, suburban homes to the yard full of fantastically carved stone work. Jodi even takes a photo of drying yellow corn next to a blue blanket. We take many shadow photos of the three of us, as well as friends from breakfast who pass us on a hill.

Nearing the city, we climb down wide stone steps, cross a narrow wooden foot bridge over the freeway and enter the city. I am filled with a mixture of curiosity, wonder and a dash of dread. I don't want this journey to end, and it's almost over. I'm curious about Santiago, the cathedral and the mass. I feel a sense of wonder in the accomplishment of achieving such a crazy goal.

A few years ago I walked 41 miles in one day to raise funds for a non-profit and thought that was a big deal. Now, after 500 miles, it seems . . . easy? Like I could do it again, tomorrow. This journey has been such an experience. On one hand, I dread it coming to an end and wonder how I will bring it forward. On the other, I am ready to get home, back to Gerald and the family. Back to the "real world." Is there such a thing?

The city seems to go on and on forever. There is no need to look at the map; we easily follow the arrows and Pilgrim traffic. At the "Santiago de Compostela" sign at the edge of the city, we ask a fellow traveler to capture the moment.

The closer we get, the greater my tension. Since we are inside the city, the guidebook doesn't help me calculate the remaining distance. It's important to me to meet up with Dale and Becky, and I'm starting to worry that I won't make it.

Santiago is filled with artwork. We stop to photograph the street graphic of a face, the star metal figurine, the amazing architecture and monuments. Traveling with artists, we stop several times to pay homage to the artists who created them. So far, everything has been modern without charm, but I know, in time, we will reach the historic center.

We continue to follow Pilgrims to the historical center of town. The closer we get, the greater my sense of urgency. The noise is deafening. I hear bagpipes, the cacophony of voices echoing off the tall buildings, and my mind is spinning. The crowd is so thick, we can barely make our way through.

The cathedral is to our left, but we are not on the "right side" to enter. After a series of left turns, we arrive at the square, Praza do Obradoiro, opposite from where we started. After the quiet of the past 37 days, it feels rushed, loud and busy. There are people everywhere, and we are wondering where to go.

Not seeing anyone we know, we head to the Pilgrim's office and find Dale sitting on a step. Seeing Dale quiets my heart. All is well. We've made it, just in time to attend the noon Pilgrim Mass. Dale has picked out good seats for us. Becky is inside, saving them. Backpacks are not allowed inside the cathedral and we don't have time to check into our hotel. Jodi offers to watch backpacks, while Thom elects to join me. Thom and I eagerly follow Dale into the magnificent cathedral.

The cathedral is shaped like a cross. We have entered on one of the short arms and make our way around to the other short side where Becky is waiting for us. In the middle of the cross is the chancel, separated from the benches by a wooden railing. Above the raised dais, stone pillars soar to an arched ceiling.

The building is packed. Pilgrims and locals, sitting on rows of beautiful worn wooden benches, wait for the ceremony to begin. The air inside is thick, heavy with anticipation.

When the ceremony begins, even though I don't understand Spanish, it feels like my soul is receiving the message without the benefit of words. I hear "You are now a Pilgrim. You come from many places and have endured many hardships to get here. But your journey has just begun. As a Pilgrim, it is your duty to go forth, to share the love of Christ with others. You are forevermore a Pilgrim."

I'm not sure what is happening, but in the middle of this beautiful message, I have to leave. It's an urge that I can't deny. I wait until the priest is finished, and then rise to leave. The look of horror on Dale's face makes me sad, but I feel compelled to go, and go NOW. The exit takes me to the far side of the building from where Jodi is waiting. Back outside, I race-walk around to her, unsure of why, but honoring the need for speed.

Climbing the steps to meet her, I see Dennis and immediately know my exit was Divine timing. It makes total sense that I felt pulled to leave. Dennis and I met on Day Six, thirty-one days ago. It was the day I climbed the Hill of Forgiveness and left Sheelagh in Uterga because I had extra energy in my legs. Two hours later, I staggered into Puente la Reina and introduced myself to Dennis at dinner. We have been energetically finding each other from the very beginning.

After the mass, Thom, Dale and Becky join us and hesitantly share that I missed the swinging of the Botafumeiro. The Botafumeiro is the silver incense burner that takes six monks pulling on a rope to swing it across the expanse of the cathedral. I was really looking forward to seeing it swing, but I'm content that I left to find my friend. You can't go wrong when you follow your heart.

The irony is I lost my cool with Thom and Jodi this morning. Between our stops to take in the art, bathroom breaks, detour to find an ATM machine, I was afraid we were going to be late to the Pilgrim Mass. Then I bagged out in the middle of the service! Sigh. I hated to disappoint Dale, and I'm sorry that I was short with Thom and Jodi. Then I remember I'm always in the right place at the right time.

We make plans to meet in the square at 6:00 to pick a location for dinner. Everyone scatters in different directions to take care of their respective business. After finding our hotel, we make our way towards the square to find a place to eat. We locate a promising restaurant but cannot tolerate the loud noises and fishy smells on the inside. So we ask to be seated at one of the tables outside. We are alone in our choice, and in looking at the patrons, I see we are the only Pilgrims. In minutes, a familiar blonde comes around the corner. Sheelagh! I jump up to hug her and we hold each other for a heart-to-heart bear-hug. We're both so happy to be together again. She's on the hunt for a room but willing to share a celebratory beer with us. Hearing her dilemma, our waitress whips out a phone, makes a call and finds Sheelagh exactly what she's looking for. We invite Sheelagh to join us for lunch, but she wants to find her room and get settled. Maybe she'll join us later for dinner.

After Sheelagh leaves, we enjoy a delicious meal filled with laughter and talk about *what just happened.* There are so many thoughts and feelings to sort through. Including, where we go from here. My flight home was booked before I came, but I do have several days left. Thom and Jodi have another three weeks to travel Portugal and Spain.

We discuss walking to Finisterre, but then dismiss the idea. The Latin meaning of Finisterre literally means "end of earth" and is located on the Spanish coastline. Before Christopher Columbus sailed, it was considered the end of the world. To walk from Santiago to Finisterre is a Pilgrimage in itself, and one that many Pilgrims do.

If we walk to Finisterre, it will be a push for me to make my plane home. My body has done what I asked of it. The idea of walking another 100 km puts my body in revolt. I can hear my feet yelling, *Enough is Enough!*

We spend the afternoon sitting in the square, surrounded by fellow travelers. Some, I will never see again. Others have become Facebook friends from around the world. Australia, Korea, Germany and Italy. Dennis and I have already exchanged our contact information. He is a friend for life. Sheelagh already had a trip planned for Texas in a few weeks with a friend, and I've invited them to visit. My Irish Camino angel is also a friend for life.

I didn't feel my journey was complete when I entered the square. I didn't feel a swell of emotion attending the Pilgrim Mass either. But when we're standing in line to receive our Compostela, Jodi gives me her beautifully painted hat for my birthday. I am flooded with emotion. I'm transported back to the café, where I feel love, loved and loving. I'm raw, vulnerable and real. I cry like a baby.

Jodi had elaborately planned the whole thing from the beginning and tricked me by getting me to sign the hat first. Each time Jodi saw someone familiar, she asked them to sign the hat. She rounded up more than twenty signatures just for me. All my Camino angels who signed it were in on the story. I have never received a gift of such pure love.

The Camino is a journey of love. Our life is a journey of love. The Camino is a gift I gave to myself. The end of the 500-mile journey is not the end. It is a doorway to new beginning.

About the Author

Cindy Arledge has enjoyed adventure from an early age. She has swum with sharks, jumped out of an airplane, and earned her Bachelor's and Master's degrees in Business as a single mother. After graduating magna cum laude, Cindy married her third husband, Gerald Fritz. They created a blended household that included three teenage girls and two dogs. In addition, they became business partners buying, renovating and selling real estate.

In 2001, Gerald and Cindy sold their business. Gerald managed their real estate while Cindy joined corporate America. Within a few years, all three of their daughters were out of the house and attending college. Life was great, until 2005.

With little warning, Cindy was plunged into "the dark night of the soul." Her beloved parents passed away within eight months of each other, and Cindy found herself at the center of a family feud. As co-executrix, she made the painful choice to leave her career to manage the day-to-day operations of her parents' commercial real estate business. Health issues ensued. Relatively debt free prior to her parents' death, Gerald and Cindy made the heart-thumping choice to borrow several million dollars to settle her parents' estate and complete renovations on their home in 2007. And then there was the economic crash of 2008.

To climb out of the emotional and financial abyss, Cindy studied Spiritual Masters and experimented with Universal Laws. And they worked. Having experienced transformation herself, Cindy was ready to inspire others. But before she shared her ideas with others, she wanted to test her formula one more time by walking 500 miles in a foreign country by herself.

Since walking the Camino, Cindy published three books within one year. She is the visionary leader of the Legacy Family Revolution. Her company specializes in assisting business owners and financially successful families to create and implement their Legacy Family Plans.

Legacy Family Planning is a values-centered approach to estate planning that can significantly reduce wealth transfer failures. Until now, it was reserved for ultra-wealthy families. To reach her vision of helping 1,000,000 families, Cindy knew it would take an army of experienced professionals. To meet the growing demand of this new industry, Cindy spearheaded the creation of The Legacy Family Planners Association (LFPA), an organization dedicated to training and certifying Legacy Family Planning professionals.

An active philanthropist, Cindy helped raise over $3 million dollars to build a women's shelter in Boerne, TX. She divides her time between her Texas Hill Country ranch that she enjoys with her husband and her "crazy grandma" house in north Texas where she goes to play with her four grandchildren.

Motivate and Inspire Others

Share a printed copy of this book.

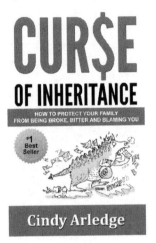

Retail: $20.00

Special Quantity Discounts

5 – 20 books	$17.50
21 – 49 Books	$ 9.95
50 + Books	$ 6.50

To place an order, contact:
210-414-7522
www.LegacyFamilyRevolution.com
info@LegacyFamilyRevolution.com

Available for Purchase
in 2017

THE
LEGACY FAMILY
WAY

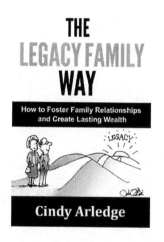

**How to Foster Family Relationships
and Create Lasting Wealth**

Cindy Arledge

Legacy Families are society's smallest and strongest economic units that thrive in the winds of change. In her latest book, The Legacy Family Way, Cindy Arledge provides a step-by-step process for creating a unified family culture based on a foundation of values, mission, and vision. Transferring gratitude and stewardship before inheritance is the secret to creating lasting wealth. This book is a must have for any business owner or financially successful family who wants to provide for their family's long-term prosperity.

To place an order, contact:
210-414-7522
www.LegacyFamilyRevolution.com
info@LegacyFamilyRevolution.com

Hire Cindy to Speak
at Your Event!

Are you looking for an attention-grabbing keynote speaker who will deliver a fresh new idea with a powerful message that adds to the success of your people?

Cindy Arledge is a dynamic humorous speaker who engages with her audiences. Whether she is sharing her inspiring Camino story or Legacy Family Planning, you're not only securing a profoundly impactful part of your program, you're investing in the long-term success of your people and their family's future.

For more info, visit

www.LegacyFamilyRevolution.com

or call +1 (210) 414-7522 today.

Are your seeking an exciting new business opportunity?

One that will help others?

Consider joining the growing number
of professional advisors.

Monthly Certification Classes
Limited Spaces Available

A Business with Purpose

For more information, contact:
210-414-7522
www.LegacyFamilyRevolution.com
info@LegacyFamilyRevolution.com